IMAGES
of America

HOT SPRINGS
FROM CAPONE TO COSTELLO

DE SOTO AT THE MISSISSIPPI.—THE REVIEW.

This early rendering shows the Spanish explorer Hernando De Soto on his quest for gold in what would become the southern United States. His travels took him west into an area that the Native Americans referred to as "the valley of the vapors." Centuries later, it would be known as Hot Springs, Arkansas. (Courtesy of Mary D. Hudgins Collection. Special Collections, University of Arkansas Libraries, Fayetteville.)

ON THE COVER: The interior of the Southern Club is seen around 1960. This photograph would have violated the policies of the Hot Springs gambling establishment, as gambling was not, and has never been, legal in Arkansas. From 1927 until 1967, however, gambling was wide open and discussed in major American publications. The photographer of this telling scene is unknown. (Courtesy of the Gangster Museum of America collection.)

IMAGES
of America

HOT SPRINGS
FROM CAPONE TO COSTELLO

*To Zoë's
Best of Luck
Bob Raines*

Robert K. Raines

ARCADIA
PUBLISHING

Published by Arcadia Publishing
Charleston, South Carolina

Printed in the United States of America

Library of Congress Control Number: 2013935757

For all general information, please contact Arcadia Publishing:
Telephone 843-853-2070
Fax 843-853-0044
E-mail sales@arcadiapublishing.com
For customer service and orders:
Toll-Free 1-888-313-2665

Visit us on the Internet at www.arcadiapublishing.com

To those that remain, and those departed, who have shared their firsthand accounts of the fascinating history of this city.

CONTENTS

FOREWORD

Have you ever had a seminal moment in life? Maybe you didn't call it *seminal*, but we have all had moments that refine, and sometimes transform, our lives. On February 7, 2009, I had my seminal moment. It was a Saturday in Los Angeles, and it had been raining for a week straight. I was sitting in my home office, severely depressed because I had just lost a television project I was passionate about. I was an aspiring writer/producer from New Jersey, and the project was my opus on how organized crime got organized in the 1920s and 1930s. The project, however, had just gone up in flames, with *Boardwalk Empire* holding the match! I was devastated. All of the research, all of the books read—all for nothing. And, as I shook my head, looking at the bookcase across from me, it happened. Hot Springs. Out of nowhere, Hot Springs, Arkansas, popped into my head. I remembered it being mentioned in several of those books I had read. Then, 30 Google-crazed seconds later, I found myself looking at the website of The Gangster Museum of America, located in Hot Springs. About five minutes after that, I was on the phone with Robert Raines, the owner, director, historical keeper of the flame, and the brains behind the museum. It was somewhere around the 45-minute mark in our ensuing conversation that I booked my flight to Hot Springs. This, of course, was based solely on Robert's promise to be my personal tour guide. "Bring a camera, plenty of paper and a good writing pen," Robert advised me. "You're gonna need 'em." One month later, while on the front portico outside of the Arlington Hotel, I was greeted by Robert with an affectionate hug, which instantly made me feel like I'd known him my whole life.

Over the course of the next three days, I was transported back to a time and place in which America's most notorious gangsters stayed in the same decadent hotels as the nation's most powerful politicians; where Hollywood's most famous actors gambled in opulent casinos with the FBI's most wanted outlaws; and where legendary professional baseball teams like the Yankees and Red Sox soaked away spring training's aches and pains in the therapeutic "healing" waters offered by the sleepy little spa town, known to all as The City of Visitors. Hour after hour and day after day, Robert told me stories I could hardly believe were true. But, incredibly, they were. And now, he is sharing them with you. I hope you enjoy this ride through one of America's best-kept secrets as much as I have. I can tell you this much: you have one heck of a tour guide!

—Glenn P. Klekowski
Television writer/producer
Beacon Pictures
September 24, 2013

INTRODUCTION

There are few places in America that have been written about more than Hot Springs, Arkansas. As far back as the 1500s, a member of Spanish explorer Hernando DeSoto's conquistadors wrote of the area where steaming water oozed from the ground, forming pools that the natives enjoyed. The writer of these chronicles, who went by the nom de plume "the Gentleman of Elvas," tells how the band camped for a month in this mountainous region, with the men and horses recuperating and enjoying renewed health. He wrote, "In this time, the horses fattened and throve more than they had done at other places." DeSoto would move on in his quest for gold, but the group of Native Americans he left behind was known as the Caddo tribe. The Caddos were a peaceful people that legend spoke of as having been born from the steam that rose from the springs. This legend, along with the healing that other Indians experienced, led to the Caddos' domain being considered sacred.

Just a few miles north of the springs, battles were fought over control of a rich novaculite deposit the Indians used for weapons and tools. The clashes, however, would not drift into the area that the Indians referred to as the Valley of the Vapors, now known as Hot Springs, Arkansas. The valley was henceforth considered neutral territory.

Thomas Jefferson, upon hearing about the springs, commissioned an expedition, led by William Dunbar and Dr. George Hunter, to explore the area, which was part of the land that Jefferson bought from Napoleon Bonaparte. Jefferson's expenditure of $15 million for half a billion acres of land (roughly 3¢ an acre), now known as the Louisiana Purchase, was considered a bad bet by some in Washington. It would not be the last bet placed in this neck of the woods.

Hunter and Dunbar wrote in their journal about a valley in the Ouachita Mountains and its thermal waters. As their descriptions circulated, people began to settle in the area. The town was called in turn Thermopolis, Warm Springs, and Hot Springs. Each year, more and more people came to enjoy and to study the mineral-rich thermal water; those early visitors certainly needed a hot bath after traveling by horseback or stagecoach over the limited number of bone-jarring trails that led to the city. By the mid-1800s, privately owned bathhouses began to open along the east side of Hot Springs Creek and Valley Street, now known as Central Avenue. In order to settle ownership claims by private citizens who had become bathhouse entrepreneurs, the US Supreme Court in 1876 declared the claims invalid and that the land and springs on which the bathhouses were built were under federal control. The court's ruling was based on an 1835 bill signed by Andrew Jackson setting aside the land to be preserved for recreational use. The land of the hot springs essentially became the country's first national park, and Bathhouse Row as we know it today was officially opened for business.

One of the most tumultuous times in American history, the Civil War, would test the neutrality of the valley, as both North and South sent soldiers to convalesce in the hot springs. As it had done with the warring tribes of Indian nations, the thermal waters overwhelmed any feelings of animosity the two sides had, and more than just broken bones and gunshot wounds were given time to heal.

Stephen Crane, author of *The Red Badge of Courage*, who was then a freelance writer for Eastern newspapers, rode the Diamond Jo Express into Hot Springs in 1895. "As soon as the train reaches the great pine belt of Arkansas one becomes aware of the intoxication of the resinous air. It is heavy, fragrant with the odor from the vast pine tracts and its subtle influence contains a prophecy of the spirit of the little city afar in the hills. Tawny roads, the soil precisely the hue of a lion's mane, wander through the groves. Nearer the town a stream of water that looks like a million glasses of lemon phosphate brawls over the rocks."

The tracks on which Crane's train traveled were built by tycoon Joseph "Diamond Jo" Reynolds, who had come to Hot Springs to seek treatment for his rheumatism years earlier. The journey by rail at that time ended in Malvern, and Reynolds experienced much travail on the bumpy road between Malvern and Hot Springs. A New Yorker who came west to make his fortune, Diamond Jo was a successful Mississippi River steamboat operator who kept the company of America's wealthiest industrialists, such as the Vanderbilts, Carnegies, and Rockefellers. He thus had no problem building a railroad that would open the gates of the spa city to the masses.

Crane continued his exposé, describing the thoroughfare that winds through the city to this day:

The motive of this Main Street [Central Avenue] is purely cosmopolitan. It undoubtedly typifies the United States, better than does any existing thoroughfare; for it resembles the North and the South, the East and the West. For a moment a row of little wooden stores will look exactly like a portion of a small prairie village, but, later, one is confronted by a group of austere business blocks that are completely Eastern in expression. The street is bright at times with gaudy gypsy coloring; it is gray in places with dull and Puritanical hues. It is wealthy and poor; it is impertinent and courteous. It apparently comprehends all men and all moods and has little to say of itself. It is satisfied to exist without being defined or classified.

When these eloquent words spread across the land, and descriptions of the healing properties of the water circulated, the rich and the poor alike began to flow in. Some came to get into the hot water, and some came to get out of hot water.

One

THE HOT WATER

People flocked to Hot Springs for many different reasons. Some came to rehabilitate in the giant Army and Navy Hospital that sits behind Bathhouse Row.

Civil War veterans Col. Samuel Fordyce and Gen. John H. Logan, both Yankees, and Dr. Algernon Garnett, a Confederate surgeon, established the military hospital at Hot Springs. General Logan had come to the spa suffering from debilitating illnesses, and his recovery was so complete that he wanted other ailing veterans to benefit from the healing waters. "Black Jack" Logan, a war hero, founder of Memorial Day, and a senator from Illinois, had little trouble pushing a bill through Congress on June 30, 1882, establishing an Army and Navy hospital. The structure, built on 24 acres of reservation land, was opened for use in January 1887.

Senator Logan would not be the only "Black Jack" to play a role in the Hot Springs saga, for across from the bathhouses, on the west side of Central Avenue, the game of blackjack was entertaining those waiting to take a bath and those who had just taken one. The only other state of being in Hot Springs at that time was actually to be in the bath. Gambling had been in the "DNA" of Hot Springs from the beginning of the settlement. Former Old West–style saloons became sophisticated dining, drinking, and entertainment venues, and dry goods stores became retail shops, pharmacies, and theaters. By the end of the century, clubs like the Arkansas Club, Indiana Club, the Kentucky Club, the Ohio Club, and, most notably, the Southern Club, were thriving on the west side of the avenue. Outside the city limits, along the main entrance to the springs from Little Rock, stood the Chicago Inn, which would later become Club Belvedere. Farther out, in Fountain Lake, was Arbor Dale.

The amenities in Hot Springs grew exponentially, as did the number of people who visited the area. Hotels and cottages sprang from the ground almost as quickly as did the water. Toward the end of the century, colossal properties, such as the Arlington and the Eastman Hotels, bookended Bathhouse Row. The Arlington Hotel, now in its third incarnation on Central Avenue, remains as the flagship of all lodging in the valley. The Pullman, the Como, the Goddard, the Marquette, the Richmond, the Ritter, the Hatterie, and the Illinois hotels all served Central Avenue. And above almost every business along the thoroughfare (with the exception of the national park bathhouses) were rooms and boardinghouses offering some semblance of accommodations for travelers spending the night. Some travelers, however, were spending more than just the night; they were spending time with ladies engaged in the world's oldest profession.

In the early years, madam Grace Goldstein operated the Hatterie Hotel, which stood on the property that now is the Arlington's valet parking garage. A businesswoman known as Josephine Belmont from New Orleans operated a bordello called the West End Hotel just off of Central Avenue on Whittington Avenue. Madam Belmont catered mostly to the professional baseball players who were in the city for spring training, while Goldstein served the more notorious elements of society, such as gamblers and outlaws. Evelyn Anderson ran the Pigley Room. Her bordello was in the triangle formed by Bridge Street, Central Avenue, and Malvern Avenue, an area known today as Spencer's Corner. Down Malvern Avenue, also known as "Black Broadway," "Mama Carrie" serviced the many jazz musicians and wealthy black men who came to enjoy the Woodmen of the Union Hotel. Prostitution became a multimillion-dollar business in Hot Springs, but while the stucco was still drying on the walls of sin city, the "sophisticrats" were busy building a more refined cosmopolitan playground. Theaters such as The Lyric, and grand stages such as The Hot Springs Opera House added culture to Central Avenue and drew New York's theater elite, such as Flo Ziegfeld and Lillian Russell. The Opera House hosted major gatherings in addition to its stage presentations.

In the spring of 1914, 300 church leaders and clergy came to the Grand Opera House at 200 Central Avenue to discuss forming an alliance of faith. The conclave adjourned a week later with the news that they had formed the Assemblies of God. Many churches of all denominations would be built in Hot Springs. One of the first Presbyterian churches in the state, First Presbyterian, stands at the corner of Central and Whittington Avenues, and St. Mary's Catholic Church was within a stone's throw on Central Avenue. By the turn of the 20th century, every race, color, and creed would be represented in Hot Springs.

While the baptismal pools were filling up with the natural thermal water, a new revenue stream had formed in this bedrock of natural beauty. Springwater bubbling from the ground was not exclusive to Bathhouse Row. Hot and cold springs were everywhere, especially in Mountain Valley, just northwest of Highway 7, and in Sleepy Valley, northeast of Highway 7. Both areas bottled and distributed the delicious and healthy mineral water all over the country. Mountain Valley Spring Water was locally owned and operated, but Chewaulka Mineral Springs Company had its home office at 3300 North Jackson Avenue in Chicago. The territory between these two springs provided the city with the fourth facet of its diamond reputation—moonshine. The cool, crystal clear, 100-proof whiskey came straight from what was known as the Possum Kingdom. Although the site of production had no formal address, everyone knew its location: an area that stretched from Belvedere to Fountain Lake and west to Jessieville. Songs and poems were penned about the Possum Kingdom. The first two stanzas of Fred Mark Palmer's "Hilltop Manor" read:

> One can go up Park Avenue, twelve, thirteen blocks, the old Highway 5,
> You're in green forest, the dark corner, a magical place long, long ago.
> Then you see rock walls, for ancient estates, then the Gorge Road and Sleepy Valley.
> You can feel history, romance and legend, and have entered the Possum Kingdom.
> The land of secrets and genuine hill people, Scotts, Irish, German and Anglo Cherokee,
>   say and know nothing—mountain folk.
> Alcohol made so clear, mineral water here, Mountain Valley and Sleepy Water, all the
>   way to Jessieville. 28 smokes, The Kingdom.

Each still, or smoke, as they called it, had its own taste, depending on the mineral content in the nearby creek and, of course, its own special recipe. Old-timers boast of no fewer than 600 camps in the Possum Kingdom. A customer had only to place a quarter on a freshly cut tree stump, walk away for a few minutes, and, upon returning, find a pint of clear liquid entertainment.

It will never be known, nor is it important, whether Johnny Torrio and young Al Capone were lured to the valley by the high-quality shine, illegal gambling, hot thermal baths, prostitution, or more mundane business opportunities. The citizenry was glad they came and welcomed them with open arms.

Entrepreneur John Cyrus Hale was credited with building one of the first bathhouses, pictured here. Hale acquired the property through squatter's rights. It would not be long before he had plenty of competition on Bathhouse Row, including from the US government.

Early bathhouses consisted of little more than a pavilion built over open-air springs. On the 400 yards of the east side of Hot Springs Creek, 60 different springs or fountains of hot water could be found. The aches and pains of the sick and weary trumped any modesty. Those seeking relief bathed together in the pools.

Charles N. Rockafellow, a colonel in the 17th Illinois Regiment, came to Hot Springs after the Civil War and established the first pharmacist-owned, stand-alone drugstore in the city, in 1866. It was located at 209 Central Avenue, across the street from the first Arlington Hotel. An 1869 advertisement read, "Fine selection of Pure Drugs and Chemicals, Patent Medicines, Soap and Toilet Articles. Prescriptions carefully compounded, day or night. For Prescriptions at night ring the bell."

The first Army and Navy Hospital is visible in the background (upper right) in this photograph of the Rammelsberg Bathhouse. Also called the "brick bathhouse," it was built around 1884. The structure was demolished in 1911 to make way, the following year, for the Buckstaff Bathhouse, located on Central Avenue.

The Hot Springs Railroad, nicknamed "the Diamond Jo," brought tourists from everywhere to Hot Springs by way of Malvern, Arkansas, where Pullman service ended. It made the three-hour scenic trip, a mere 25–30 miles as the crow flies, under the power of a wood-burning locomotive (above) that ran on narrow-gauge track. The journey, slow and bumpy, was an improvement on the former means of transportation into the valley, stage line or horseback. In 1890, Joseph Reynolds upgraded his tracks to a wider gauge, allowing him to utilize the larger, more elegant Pullman cars for a more comfortable trip to the increasingly popular tourist destination. Reynolds's transportation monopoly ended when direct service from Little Rock was built at the turn of the century. Eventually, the Missouri Pacific Lines (below) absorbed these smaller rail connections.

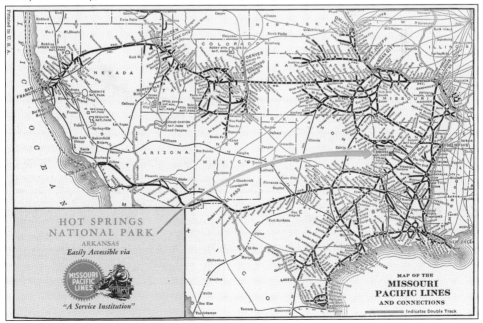

The Indiana Club, a gambling hall at 426 1/2 Central Avenue, was best known not for its successes but for one of its failures. In 1913, wealthy, well-connected Indianapolis businessman Frank Fox was duped out of $20,000. The uproar he created, from the mayor's office all the way to the governor, led to a moratorium on gambling for the next several years. (Courtesy of Garland County Historical Society.)

The Kentucky Club stood at 314 Central Avenue. It was a gambling hall and bar that also housed a bordello in the upper rooms, which was common for the clubs of the day. The Kentucky, along with the Ohio, the Belvedere, and the Southern, was part of the gambling empire owned by W.S. Jacobs. (Courtesy of Garland County Historical Society.)

The Ohio Club, at 336 Central Avenue, was built directly across the street from Bathhouse Row. With large gaming tables and slots, it was primarily a gambling hall through the years, but it became a cigar store during Prohibition. It soon returned to business as usual, and it was a favorite haunt of Al Capone and his boys. It contains a massive hand-carved mahogany bar and back bar that was cut in half and floated down the Mississippi River, to be installed in the Hot Springs establishment upon its opening in 1903. The Ohio Club stands today as the oldest tavern in Arkansas. (Right, courtesy of Special Collections, University of Arkansas, Fayetteville; below, courtesy of Mike Pettey.)

Built in 1893, the Southern Club was a popular gambling and entertainment establishment located across Central Avenue from the Arlington Hotel. Arguably the most popular club in the downtown area, it underwent many renovations through the years with each change in ownership. Its most dramatic upgrade came in the late 1920s, when dark Pittsburgh glass was added to the front of the building. Perhaps its most famous customer, Al Capone, began his regular appearances at the poker table during this same time. According to one well-known story, "Big Al" paid a cab driver $100 to make the U-turn that would take him back to his residence, directly across the street at the Arlington. In later years, a childhood friend of Capone's was seen daily at the Southern. That person was Owen Vincent Madden, a New York gangster who became a prominent Hot Springs retiree. Madden was at the Southern often enough that most people thought he owned the establishment; in fact, his wife's name did appear on later deeds of title.

The Belvedere Club stood on 40 acres of a 1,000-acre farm about four miles northeast of Hot Springs, on Highway 7 North, the old stagecoach route from Little Rock to Hot Springs. Originally the Chicago Inn, the Belvedere opened and held its first gala on Valentine's Day, 1929. Under the ownership of W.S. Jacobs, who also ran the Belvedere Dairy on the property, the Belvedere Club had crystal chandeliers, elegant, spacious dining areas, a casino, and a bar. Through the years, it hosted guests such as Al and Ralph Capone and their entourage; heavyweight champion Jack Dempsey and his wife, Estelle Taylor; jazz greats Callie Dill and Louis Jordan; and other celebrities and athletes, such as major-league baseball players and movie stars. (Courtesy of the Fred Mark Palmer Collection.)

Since 1875, the Arlington Hotel has been the hallmark of luxury hotels in Hot Springs, and remains to this day the largest in Arkansas. A colonial porch ran the full length of the building. The graceful, wooden structure was three stories tall, had 120 rooms, and was illuminated by gaslights. A grand lobby structurally connected the two wings. In the late 1880s, a 100-room annex and a new dining room with electric lights were added. The hotel was built on federal reservation property (now known as Arlington Park). (Courtesy of Mary D. Hudgins Collection. Special Collections, University of Arkansas Libraries, Fayetteville.)

On February 8, 1892, the Arlington Hotel Company was legally formed, and a decision was made to raze the wooden Arlington and replace it with a larger, brick structure, at a cost of $550,000. The second Arlington, with a guest capacity of 500, opened in the spring of 1893. The hotel was totally destroyed by fire in 1923. (Courtesy of Mary D. Hudgins Collection, Special Collections, University of Arkansas Libraries, Fayetteville.)

Construction on the present-day Arlington (right) began in 1923, and it opened with a gala on New Year's Eve 1924. No longer on federal property, across Fountain street, the 478-room luxury resort hotel offered amenities such as an Arthur Murray Dance Studio, a roof garden, a bathhouse with its own elevator, a full-service gas station/automobile repair shop, cigar/newsstand, board of trade, Western Union office, stenographers, laundry, drugstore, commercial print shop, barber and beauty salon, around-the-clock medical staff, grand ballroom, and 10-piece orchestra. Through the years, it has been the hotel of choice for the famous and infamous, including Al Capone, Lucky Luciano, Ben Siegel, Meyer Lansky, and Titanic Thompson. Giants of industry, such as Andrew Carnegie, F.W. Woolworth, and the Rockefellers, along with politicians such as presidents Franklin Roosevelt, Harry Truman, Ronald Reagan, and John F. Kennedy, all enjoyed the resort's amenities. Athletes like Jack Dempsey, Rocky Marciano, and Babe Ruth, and celebrities such as Rudolph Valentino, Elizabeth Taylor, and Marilyn Monroe made the Arlington their own private getaway. (Courtesy of Mary D. Hudgins Collection, Special Collections, University of Arkansas Libraries, Fayetteville.)

The Eastman Hotel, located on Reserve Street across from the Army and Navy Hospital, was known as "the Monarch of the Glen." Its 520 rooms and 12-foot-wide hallways resulted in a promenade 675 feet long. The hotel catered to families and was known for its social gatherings and musical entertainment. Owned by some of the directors of the Arlington Hotel, the Eastman was "home plate" for most of the major-league baseball players participating in spring training held in Hot Springs. Babe Ruth became a familiar face around town, having trained in the city for nine seasons. The Babe's salary dispute with the Yankees was settled at the Eastman with the flip of a coin. Walter Johnson, upon returning to the city after his 1925 World Series win, entertained hotel guests by warming up his pitching arm on the lawn. (Courtesy of Mary D. Hudgins Collection. Special Collections, University of Arkansas Libraries, Fayetteville.)

The Hotel Pullman was a 100-room, Mediterranean-style hotel that stood at 504 Central Avenue, across from the Buckstaff Bathhouse. The Pullman claimed to be the most popular hotel outside "the big four" (the Majestic, the Arlington, the Eastman, and the Park), and it advertised itself as "the Gem of The Valley." (Courtesy of Garland County Historical Society.)

Built at the junction of Central, Ouachita, Market, and Olive Streets, the Como Hotel took its name from the first letter of each of these streets. The hotel, which opened in 1915, was built of distinctive glazed white bricks produced by Leon Tiffany, the brother of the famed New York jeweler. (Courtesy of Historical Attractions Inc.)

The original structure of the Majestic Hotel (left of center) was built in 1903 on the homesite of Horace Whittington, one of the city's founding fathers. It expanded westward, with a new annex (left) opening in December 1926. Guests enjoyed rooms that opened into the mountainside and a pool at the base of the mountain. A glass wall enabled guests to view the luxurious pool area from the mezzanine. It was this view of the pool that many historians claim was Ben "Bugsy" Siegel's inspiration to create a similar setting when he began construction of the Flamingo Hotel in Las Vegas. The hotel played host to many grand galas, including the wedding of Augustus Busch. Perhaps the property's most infamous guest was George "Bugs" Moran, the Chicago rival and enemy of Al Capone. Both resided in Hot Springs concurrently, with Moran staying at the Majestic while Capone's outfit stayed at the Arlington. Hot Springs was the only place in America where these two warring factions could be in such close proximity without shots being fired. (Courtesy of Mary D. Hudgins Collection, Special Collections, University of Arkansas Libraries, Fayetteville.)

The Supreme Lodge of the Woodmen of Union, a black social club/fraternity, built the National Baptist Hotel at 501 Malvern Avenue in 1923. The building, in close proximity to Central Avenue, housed a 100-bed hospital, a 75-room bath hotel, a bank, and a 2,500-seat auditorium that attracted such performers as Count Basie and Duke Ellington. Due to the many black jazz legends who performed here, Malvern Avenue was nationally known as Black Broadway. The hotel was the epicenter for the Policy Kings, who ruled the numbers rackets in Chicago and New York. The prime ministers of the black underworld had a common expression when making deals: "Meet me in Hot Springs." Black gangsters like Bumpy Johnson, Ted Roe, and the Jones brothers were frequent visitors. It is said that the assassination of Roe was planned in Hot Springs by his black counterparts, and that the contract was given to Sam Giancano. Black racketeers knew that the quickest way to gain prestige in the underworld was to be seen in Hot Springs. (Courtesy of Garland County Historical Society.)

On the second floor of the building known today as Spencer's Corner, Evelyn Anderson and Daisy Cooner operated the Pigley Rooms, a house of prostitution for more than 65 years. Built in the trapezoid block formed at Broadway, Bridge Street, and Central Avenue, the building has survived major downtown fires. It housed the Bridge Club, an illegal casino. (Courtesy of Historical Attractions Inc.)

At the corner of Whittington and Central Avenues on the north end of the downtown area, workmen replace a section of the trolley track that ran south from Whittington Park, down Central Avenue, to Oaklawn Park Race Track. In the background is First Presbyterian Church, built in 1907. (Courtesy of Historical Attractions Inc.)

The doors of the Grand Opera House opened in 1882 at 200 Central Avenue. Attendance reached its peak in 1902, when over 190 performances were held. Legendary performers such as Lillian Russell, John Barrymore, and Billie Burke appeared in productions at the opera house. Attractions from minstrel shows to grand opera entertained crowds in the 1,000-seat theater. Florenz Ziegfeld, with his common-law wife, Anna Held, attended performances at the venue after taking in the baths, according to local historians. Held (below, center) led a traveling chorus line that would later become the Ziegfeld Girls. The facility also served civic purposes, but by far the most important event that took place at the opera house was the formation of the Assemblies of God Church. (Above, courtesy of GCHS; below, courtesy of the Fred Mark Palmer Collection.)

THE CHORUS IN "THE LITTLE DUCHESS," WITH MISS ANNA HELD IN THE CENTRE

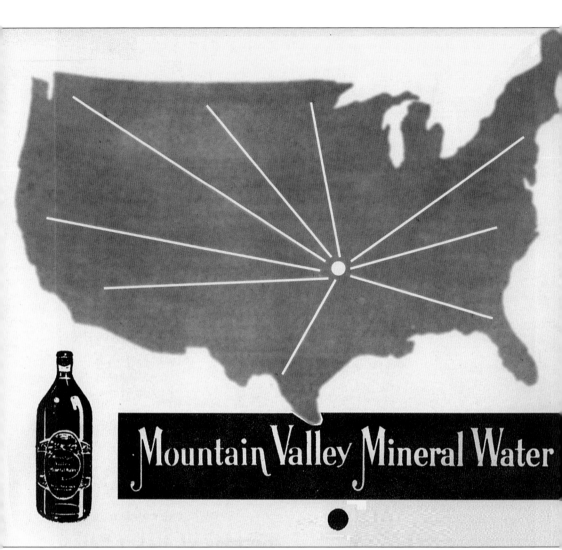

Water from Lockett's Spring, located 12 miles north of Hot Springs at the base of Blakely Mountain, had been sold locally as Lockett's Spring Water until 1871, when pharmacist Peter Greene bought the property and began to sell the now-famous Mountain Valley Spring Water. Greene and his brother John opened the Mountain Valley Resort Hotel in 1875. The water and resort were named after Mountain Valley, a nearby community. Mountain Valley Water holds the distinction of being one of the first companies to franchise in America. It first appeared at the White House in the 1920s, when Calvin Coolidge served the healthy springwater. Other notables who enjoyed its health benefits were US senators, Elvis Presley, heavyweight boxing champion Joe Louis, and scores of major-league baseball players who trained in Hot Springs. Enjoyment of the water has not been limited to human overachievers. Thoroughbreds such as Secretariat, Kelso, Bold Ruler, and Sunday Silence were trained on this famous springwater. (Courtesy of Historical Attractions Inc.)

TO RETAIN OR REGAIN HEALTH DRINK

Sleepy Water **FROM HOT SPRINGS ARKANSAS**

ORDER A CASE TODAY

TELEPHONE or write—prompt delivery will be made. Once you have tried this marvelous natural health adjuster, you will never be without it. Order a case for your home and one for your place of business, too; so that you may drink Sleepy Water at all times during the day. Put yourself on a six weeks' test with Sleepy Water and note the remarkably beneficial results.

DIRECTIONS

Sleepy Water is effective only when taken abundantly and with regularity. As an ordinary health protective measure, drink at least 8 glasses per day. For the treatment of a diseased condition, a full gallon daily is recommended. In this case, its beneficial effects are customarily manifested after a period of eight to twelve weeks of consistently regular use.

We do not filter Sleepy Water. You get it just as it comes from the famous Chewaukla Springs. Thus the therapeutic value is undiminished—nothing is taken away.

The slight accumulation at the bottom of the bottle is *not* valueless sediment—it is a precipitate composed of natural constituents of the water. To get full value from Sleepy Water, you must, therefore, *shake the bottle well before using.*

Delivered To Your Door

Sleepy Water is available to you in your own home or place of business. Your local distributor will deliver it to your door as often as you require—12 one-half gallon bottles to a case. If there is no dealer in your community, write to us direct.

Chewaukla Mineral Springs Co.
3330 W. Jackson Blvd., Chicago
Telephone: Kedzie 1228

Drink at Least 8 Glasses a Day

Legend tells of an Indian Chief who came to the Valley of the Vapors searching for relief. He bathed in the thermal waters, only to find that his condition worsened. In hopes of seeking a remedy for his pain, his daughter led him to cool springs she had heard had mystical powers. After drinking the water, he fell into a deep sleep and awoke cured of his ailment. From then on, he called his daughter *Chewaulka*, in celebration of his regained health. The springs were then named Chewaulka Springs, and its water became known for its relaxing and sleep-inducing effects. In the 1920s and 1930s, Chicago investors purchased the property and began extensive nationwide marketing and sales of the water. Sales climbed when Guy Lombardo released the song "Sweet Chewaulka, Land of Sleepy Water" (right). (Courtesy of GCHS.)

SWEET CHEWAUKLA

THE LAND OF SLEEPY WATER

Words by
FRED C. HIGMAN
Music by
CARMEN LOMBARDO

featured by
Guy Lombardo and his Orchestra

Irving Berlin, Inc.
MUSIC PUBLISHERS
1607 Broadway New York

Moonshining got its name from the early British, who were illegally distilling alcoholic spirits under the "shine of the moon." In America, those who distributed the "shine" were called bootleggers, because, initially, they concealed the distillate in high-legged boots. Many remote areas of America had moonshiners and bootleggers, but the area north of Hot Springs known as the Possum Kingdom brewed a distinctive product called "clear" because of the clear mountain mineral water used for the mash. This facility used a process that combined corn (or cornmeal), water, yeast, and heat. Malt was added to accelerate the fermentation process. The steam that rose from this alchemy dripped through a spiraling copper tube known as a "worm" into a jug, and the product was stored for distribution in different-sized bottles. At one time, Hot Springs had four bottling plants that did nothing but make bottles. The need for moonshine grew exponentially due to Prohibition, and this may be why Johnny Torrio, Al Capone, and Joe Kennedy took a shining to Hot Springs. (Courtesy of Historical Attractions Inc.)

Two

BIG AL COMES TO TOWN

In the early 1920s, Johnny Torrio and his wife, along with his protégé Al Capone, first stayed at the Eastman Hotel. According to local newspaper accounts, they checked into the hotel as Mr. and Mrs. Frank Langley and Al Brown. Their aliases were well-known among newspaper reporters of the time. Later, Capone's whiskey-hauling trucks would bear the name Al Brown's Used Furniture. Torrio would find himself under attack from his gangland rivals when he returned to the Windy City after vacationing in Hot Springs. Soon, he would relinquish control and turn over "The Chicago Outfit" to young Alphonse Capone.

In the meantime, Hot Springs was about to elect a mayor who would set the stage for the arrival of Capone and many more like him. Leo Patrick McLaughlin was elected mayor of this sleepy little valley town in 1927, and over the next 20 years, he would get things very organized with a little help from his friends. During McLaughlin's campaign, he remarked that, if elected, he would "open the town up." Everyone knew that he was talking about gambling, and many felt this was the path to prosperity for the city. It would take McLaughlin a few years to get his political machine rolling, but, before long, the police department, the fire department, and all city employees were making money off of the gambling operation. Having served several terms as city attorney prior to 1927, McLaughlin had a vast knowledge of how the city operated. Little did the public know that Leo P. McLaughlin had never taken the bar exam and, in fact, had attended the University of Arkansas for only two weeks. He would end up practicing law in Hot Springs for 45 years.

When Al Capone returned to Hot Springs with his newly found entourage, he set up operations on the fourth floor of the Arlington Hotel. Hot Springs would be the perfect resort for the young crime boss, for it had all the amenities Capone enjoyed: golf, gambling, drinking during Prohibition, spring training for major-league baseball teams, thermal baths, and, of course, prostitution. Capone's visits to the city were always an exciting time for those in the hospitality industry as well as for tourists. For planned visits, Capone would normally ship his armored 1928 Cadillac by way of the Rock Island Rail and the Missouri Pacific Railroad, so that while he was in Hot Springs, he could drive around town in style. Many legends were passed on from Arlington employees to their children and are still reported today. One such legend, perhaps a true story, was told by an Arlington housekeeper, Aunt Bessie. Capone would rent the entire fourth floor of the Arlington so that each man in his 40-man traveling party would know who his neighbor was. On one occasion, Aunt Bessie returned to her cart in the hallway after cleaning one of Capone's many adjoining suites. She then moved the cart to the next doorway, used her pass key, and opened the door to the room. Upon entering, the men who were playing cards in the room she had just left drew their weapons, freezing Aunt Bessie in her tracks. Capone entered from an adjoining room, and the men relaxed their weapons. Capone gave Aunt Bessie a $100 bill and reminded her to always reenter the room she had just left through the same doorway while he was in residence.

Al Capone was known to be generous and polite to everyone he met in Hot Springs, and it was possibly the only place in America he could visit without being concerned for his safety or the responsibility of running a business.

Capone enjoyed the Hot Springs nightlife, spending most of his time at the Belvedere Club, The Southern Club, and the Ohio Club, along with the Arlington lobby. The Belvedere may have meant more to Capone than just recreation. Capone family members and even some historians believe that he and Joe Kennedy used the Belvedere Dairy to manufacture crystal clear moonshine, slip the elixir into Mountain Valley water bottles and kegs, and ship the shine all over the country in Mountain Valley trucks and railcars. It is interesting to note that Mountain Valley became the National Water of Congress in the late 1920s.

Capone did not return to the spa city after 1930, due to his tax evasion trial. After Capone's incarceration in 1931, Frank Nitti assumed control of the Outfit and continued the pilgrimage to Hot Springs. Nitti and his second wife adopted a baby from an orphanage on Malvern Avenue. After his brother's incarceration, Ralph Capone returned many times to the city that he and his brother referred to as "Bubbles." Historians believe the code word was chosen due to the champagne that flowed and the many baths that were taken. Ralph Capone loved Oaklawn Park Thoroughbred Race Track and frequented the area during the live race meets. When visiting Hot Springs, Ralph spent a lot of his time with Emil Denemark, who owned Denemark Cadillac in Chicago and who moreover was a prominent horse owner who won several Arkansas Derbies. Denemark built the 1928 armored Cadillac for Big Al. While Al Capone and his boys enjoyed the finer things in life, like playing golf at Hot Springs Country Club, a new wave of notorious visitors would drift into the spa city: bank robbers and outlaws.

Alphonse Gabriel Caponi, later Americanized to Capone, was born on January 27, 1899, in New York City, according to family members. He dropped out of school in the sixth grade and joined one of the many street gangs in Brooklyn. The tougher and older Al Capone had, in a few years, graduated from being a juvenile delinquent to membership in The Five Points Gang, where he met Johnny Torrio, who had just gone through a similar commencement into the same gang. Capone took his first real step toward his destiny when Torrio received an invitation from an in-law, "Big Jim" Colosimo, to move to Chicago. Torrio was handed control of Colosimo's operation, which consisted of whorehouses, gambling rings, and protection rackets. He soon summoned the help of Al Capone, his Five Points gang mate. Capone left the Big Apple and headed for the Windy City. (Courtesy of William J. Helmer.)

Once Al Capone made it to Chicago and began to survey the lay of the land, he realized he was going to need some muscle to get the job done of enforcing Torrio's mandate. He called the most violent man he knew, his brother Frank (shown here), who had also been in the Five Points Gang, along with his brother Ralph. The two were summoned from New York and began assembling the team that would take over Chicago and add illegal booze to Torrio's product line, which included prostitution and gambling. Frank's motto was "a corpse never talks." Some historians believe that it could have been Frank's propensity for violence that kept him away from Hot Springs, but it was more likely his early demise from the weight of the .45 caliber lead that was pumped into him by the Chicago police on election day in 1924. His spot on the roster would be filled by another Frank, Frank Nitti. (Courtesy of William J. Helmer.)

Following Torrio's contracted killing of Dion O'Bannion, Torrio and his wife fled to Hot Springs to lie low. Within days, Torrio (right) received a report that O'Bannion's henchmen had left Chicago looking for him. The Torrios headed for New Orleans and then on to the Bahamas, Cuba, and St. Petersburg, Florida. Hoping the situation in Chicago had cooled off, they returned home. The situation had not cooled off. Torrio was ambushed by George "Bugs" Moran, hit man for the North Side Gang. Torrio miraculously recovered from his wounds and spent nine months in jail on a set-up bootlegging charge that had led to O'Bannion's death. Exhausted, Torrio summoned Al Capone (below) to his cell and turned over the South Side Gang to Capone and his family. At the age of 26, Al Capone had become the crime boss of Chicago. (Courtesy of William J. Helmer.)

One of the many things the Capone brothers (above) liked to do in Hot Springs was visit Happy Hollow Amusement Park, located north of the Arlington Hotel on Fountain Street. The Capones, along with Mae Capone, Al's wife (below), were photographed several times at Happy Hollow, as well as at another famous Hot Springs tourist attraction, The Ostrich Farm, on upper Whittington Avenue. These activities and other forms of recreation, such as the National Park Rifle Range at 220 Central Avenue, spring games between major-league baseball teams, golf at Hot Springs Country Club, and hot-water soaks, combined with gambling, alcohol, and friendly women, provided the perfect vacation for Al and his boys. (Courtesy of GCHS.)

The Belvedere Dairy, operated by W.S. Jacobs, was located on his property overlooking Johnny Torrio's favorite tavern, The Chicago Inn. The inn later became Club Belvedere, and the dairy, according to old-timers, not only produced fresh milk, but was known to have run several thousand gallons of moonshine through its pristine distillation system for Al Capone and his partner, Joe Kennedy. (Courtesy of Fred Mark Palmer.)

The 1928 armored Cadillac had one-inch-thick glass and solid rubber tires, and weighed 9,850 pounds. It was built by Emil Denemark in Chicago after an attempt on Capone's life by a rival gang member while Capone was traveling from Club Belvedere back to the Arlington. The car was shipped to Hot Springs on the Rock Island Railroad and then driven around the city during Capone's visits. (Courtesy of Historical Attractions Inc.)

READ THIS!

I WILL APPRECIATE YOUR VOTE

Leo P. McLaughlin, CANDIDATE FOR MAYOR

THIS IS THE ONLY CITY IN THE WORLD WHERE THE MAYOR DOES NOT DEVOTE HIS FULL TIME TO THE OFFICE.

I WILL DEVOTE MY FULL TIME TO THE OFFICE.

My Experience as City Attorney for Twelve Years Has Trained Me In the Affairs of the City.

The City of Hot Springs is $435,000.00 in Debt!

I Can Run the City On Its Income!

Election April 5th, 1927

Leo P. McLaughlin (left) got his feet wet in the pool of politics when he dropped out of the University of Arkansas after just two weeks of quasi-matriculation and returned to Hot Springs. He ran for city attorney and, remarkably, was elected. His claim to fame until that point was having been captain of the first Hot Springs High School basketball team, which had been introduced to the game by visiting baseball great Honus Wagner. The Supreme Court of Arkansas shows no record of Leo Patrick McLaughlin having taken the bar exam, yet he practiced law in Hot Springs for 45 years and became a very good divorce attorney. He would need these skills in the years to come, as he himself was divorced three times. Once, McLaughlin was sued by a woman in Oklahoma because he did not fulfill his promise to marry her, an offer that had apparently been made by mistake, according to McLaughlin, in a moment of passion. (Above, courtesy of Fred Mark Palmer; left, courtesy of GCHS.)

Unlike Al Capone, who was sensitive about his scars (he is shown here covering the scars that resulted from a bar fight in Coney Island in his younger days), Hot Springs would not harbor the baggage of any of its visitors. In a town that thrived on gambling and sin before Las Vegas even had water, what happened in Hot Springs dissipated with the steam that rose from the ground. (Courtesy of W.J. Helmer.)

Capone (right), seen here with attorney Abe Teitelbaum in 1941, once said, "The honest lawmakers of any city can be counted on your fingers. I could count Chicago's on one hand! Virtue, honor, truth, and the law have all vanished from our life. We are smart-alecky. We like to be able to 'get away with' things. And if we can't make a living at some honest profession, we're going to make one anyway." (Courtesy of W.J. Helmer.)

One of Ralph Capone's favorite pastimes while in Hot Springs was visiting Oaklawn Park Thoroughbred Race Track. His love of horses led him to make an offer on property north of Hot Springs on Highway 7, with plans to build a second-chance ranch for thoroughbred racehorses that could no longer compete. A deal was never reached with the owner of the property, but Ralph would continue to visit Hot Springs with his lifelong New York friend, Owney Madden. Ralph was seen several times in the company of mayor Leo P. McLaughlin in his box at Oaklawn Park and while dining at the Arlington Hotel. Ralph Capone also enjoyed playing golf at Hot Springs Country Club. James "Ev" Young, former caddie to Ralph, and Jake Guzik, a Capone insider, recalled that Capone's party was always pleasant, relaxed, and tipped very well. (Courtesy of Fred Mark Palmer.)

Hot Springs Golf and Country Club, Hot Springs National Park, Ark.

One might think that when old friends get together around a card table in the men's locker room of the Hot Springs Country Club, the conversation would be about the fledgling PGA using the club as one of its tour events, or about golf legends Paul Runyan, Ken Venturi, Cary Middlecoff, and Julius Boros walking the fairways. In fact, men who were known for things other than golf, such as Al and Ralph Capone, Frank Costello, Joe Adonis, Owney Madden, Ben Siegel, George Raft, and Meyer Lansky, seemed to always creep into the conversation. Hot Springs Country Club has been a property owned by the stockholders of the Arlington Hotel since its inception in 1898. One of its 18-hole courses is named in the hotel's honor. The other course, named "the Park course" (formerly the Majestic), is slightly longer. Both courses offer their own challenges to the golf enthusiast. (Courtesy of Historical Attractions Inc.)

If anyone could find the lighter side of Al Capone, it was Titanic Thompson. Born Clarence Thomas in Rogers, Arkansas, Titanic received his name from the colossal wagering situations that he created with his unsuspecting opponents. Titanic usually knew the outcome of the wager before the deal went down. A famous story in Thompson's biography talks of the day he defeated Capone in a round of golf at Hot Springs Country Club. Later, in the club house, having just finished his round from the right side, Thompson boasted of being able to beat the Chicago mobster left-handed. Capone took the bait, and Titanic and Capone went back on the course to play for double or nothing, a $10,000 wager. Little did Capone know that Thompson was a natural southpaw and played several strokes better from the left. Capone enjoyed Thompson's company, although he rarely won a bet against him. They were known to spend hours on the Arlington veranda, betting on everything. (Courtesy of Corbis Images.)

Three

THE OUTLAWS

As the Depression spread across the land, the Volstead Act (Prohibition) had little effect on the economy of Hot Springs. A different caliber of criminal, yet just as notorious as the Chicago Outfit, sought sanctuary in Hot Springs. The profit-minded police and politicians created a metropolitan hole in the wall for the likes of Frank Nash, Alvin Karpis, the Barker Gang, Pretty Boy Floyd, and Bonnie and Clyde. The freedom to rest, relax, and mend their wounds allowed these criminals to plan their next jobs and, more important to the Hot Springs downtown business district, to spend their hard-earned cash. Frank "Jelly" Nash was doing just that when he was arrested, or more likely kidnapped, by federal agents in the White Front Club on Central Avenue. Nash, an Arkansas native, acquired the nickname "The Gentleman Bank Robber" because of his natty dress and his politeness in illegally "withdrawing" money from banks. His arrest and subsequent transfer to Kansas City for a trip back to prison resulted in the Union Station Kansas City Massacre. Ironically, the arresting agents had requested backup from Fort Smith, Arkansas, to Kansas City for fear of some kind of an intervention by Nash's associates. The request, to J. Edgar Hoover himself, went unanswered, and so the posse and passenger continued on to Kansas City. According to most historians, upon their arrival at the Union Station railway, they were met by machine-gun fire from Charles Arthur Floyd, Vernon Miller, and Adam Richetti. During the ensuing gunfight, Nash was killed by an accidental gunshot blast from one of the agents in the rear of the car in which he was a passenger. Nash's wife, Frances, was landing nearby in a plane that had taken off at Stover Field in Hot Springs. She returned to Hot Springs, denied the opportunity to see her husband for a final time until he was laid to rest in Paragould, Arkansas.

As Nash was meeting his demise, his old friend and business associate, Alvin Karpis, was enjoying the company of his common-law wife, madam Grace Goldstein, in the Hatterie Hotel on Central Avenue. Karpis spent a lot of time in and around Hot Springs with Goldstein, mostly at 123 Palm Street and the Woodcock House, which overlooked Lake Catherine on Highway 270. Karpis was the mastermind of the Barker-Karpis Gang, and he planned jobs for the Dillinger Gang. While Alvin Karpis was on the road, practicing his trade of robbing banks and trains and kidnapping millionaires for ransom, madam Grace was sharing her "product" with the Hot Springs chief of police, Joe Wakelin, and chief of detectives, Herbert "Dutch" Akers. After Karpis's arrest in New Orleans in 1936, the trio of Goldstein, Wakelin, and Akers served time for harboring the FBI's last Public Enemy No. 1. Around this time, Bonnie Parker had been injured in a car accident in Alma, Arkansas, northwest of Hot Springs, and was brought to the spa city by Clyde Barrow to take in the healing waters. The couple stayed in the motor court on Fountain Street just northeast of the Arlington Hotel, in an amusement area called Happy Hollow. Perhaps by plan, just next door was a shooting gallery owned by Frank James, brother of Jesse. Bonnie and Clyde were known to follow the trail of the James Gang in their exploits, according to Barrow family historians. A short time later, the lovebirds would sing their final song in Gibsland, Louisiana, about 160 miles south of Hot Springs.

Charles Arthur "Pretty Boy" Floyd spent time and money in the city while taking time off from his criminal activities (what he considered his business ventures), and was known to have had a meeting with mayor Leo McLaughlin at least once. Some of Floyd's family later migrated from Oklahoma to Hot Springs, and at least one enjoyed success as a member of the Hot Springs medical community. In the meantime, while a lot of attention was being paid to these dangerous visitors, a man from New York City nicknamed "the Killer" would quietly move into town in the early 1930s and never leave.

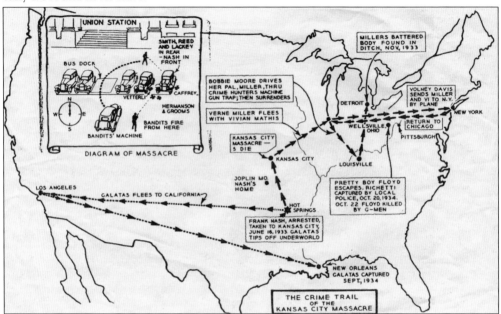

(Kansas City Massacre map courtesy of William J. Helmer.)

42

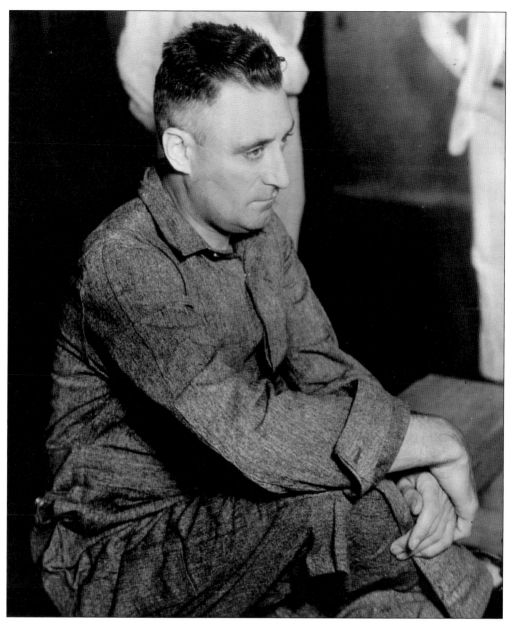

Most guests visited the Arlington Hotel to rest and relax. However, one lesser-known guest, Harvey Bailey, used his suite to plan some of the largest bank robberies in history. Emissaries from the "job site" would bring him reports, including the times police would be walking by on their beat, when money was dropped off at the bank, and when the fewest customers would be inside the building. Thus, "Old Harve," as Bailey was called due to his prematurely gray hair, orchestrated bank robberies that resulted in the highest income of any man in his profession. Among the banks Bailey robbed were Hamilton County Bank in Cincinnati, in 1922, for $265,000; the Denver US Mint, in 1923, for $500,000; and the Lincoln National Bank & Trust, in 1930, for $2,654,700. In 1933, Bailey staged a successful jail breakout with weapons supplied by Frank Nash. There were no bank robberies in Hot Springs during the times the outlaws were in town on vacation. (Courtesy of Argenta Images.)

Frank Nash was not only proficient at robbing banks, but his ability to plan and execute prison escapes gained him much respect from his peers. Nash developed the ability to, in the midst of a heist, keep everyone calm, cool, and collected. His unsuspecting looks brought surprise to bank tellers and trained personnel when he delivered the words, "Give me all your money." Through a complex network of hoodlums and safe houses, Nash, a wanted man after strolling out of Leavenworth, was able to travel between Hot Springs and Aurora, Minnesota, with relative ease. He met, fell in love with, and promised to wed a Minnesota girl, Frances Luce. They married in Hot Springs on May 25, 1933, the event witnessed and facilitated by Dick Galatas, the manager of Nash's favorite hangout in Hot Springs, the White Front Club, at 310 Central Avenue. The couple honeymooned in the spa city for a few days and headed north. They returned three weeks later, and, according to researcher Orval Allbritton, Nash was spotted in the White Front by local businessman Bill Seiz, who reported the sighting to the FBI. Nash was arrested a few days later by federal agents at the club, and the arrest resulted in the Kansas City Massacre. (Courtesy of William J. Helmer.)

In 1920, the same year that Prohibition became the law of the land, the Auto-Ordnance Company of New York contracted with the Colt's Patent Firearms Manufacturing Company of Hartford, Connecticut, to produce 15,000 Thompson submachine guns. At the time, no one knew what a submachine gun was, but, five years later, it became a worldwide symbol of American gangland violence. Intended for the Army, the tommy gun was the brainchild of Brig. Gen. John Thompson (seen here). With a small fortune already invested in the project, Auto-Ordnance tried to market the gun commercially. At demonstrations in 1920, weapons experts acclaimed its revolutionary design, reliability, and enormous firepower, and one dazzled police official predicted it would either kill or cure the country's gunmen, rioters, and "motorized bandits." But that early enthusiasm never translated into sales. In 1926, a *Collier*'s writer described it less approvingly: "This Thompson submachine gun is nothing less than a diabolical engine of death . . . the paramount example of peace-time barbarism and the diabolical acme of human ingenuity in man's effort to devise a mechanical contrivance with which to murder his neighbor." (Courtesy of William J. Helmer.)

Grace Goldstein was born Jewell LaVerne Grayson in 1905 in Paris, Texas. At the age of 19, she headed for New Orleans, where she honed her skills as a prostitute and madam before moving to Hot Springs. Her bordello was on the second and third floors of the Hatterie Hotel. The first floor was a well-known haberdashery. Goldstein would keep the company of Alvin Karpis enough to be considered his common-law wife, and in the years following his arrest, she, too, would serve time in prison, for harboring him. *The Arkansas Democrat*, in an article by Roy Bosson entitled "FBI Assault on Gangland Began in Spa," reported that Goldstein's maid provided the proceedings with its lightest moment. Questioning by US attorney Fred Isgrig began, "Do you work in a house of prostitution?" "No sir!" came the emphatic reply. Realizing the maid might not understand, he rephrased the question. "Well, do you work in a house of ill repute?" "No sir, it was a nice place." Still trying, Isgrig asked, "Well, now, isn't where you work a sporting house?" "No sir!" Isgrig asked pointedly, "Then where did you work?" "I works in a whorehouse." (Courtesy of Robert Livesy.)

The above photograph shows the residence of Grace Goldstein, 123 Palm Street, just a couple of blocks off Central Avenue. Goldstein's primary source of income was operating a bordello, located just north of the Arlington Hotel, known as The Hatterie. J.D. McClard, longtime barbeque entrepreneur in Hot Springs, recalls cooking goat and delivering it to the Palm Street address as a youngster. Years later, he realized that the fellow who paid him was none other than Alvin Karpis. The Woodcock House (right), which rested high atop a hill seven miles southeast of Hot Springs on Highway 270 East, was a hideaway for Goldstein, Karpis, and some of their closest friends, such as Connie Morris and Fred Hunter. It was here that the FBI acquired Goldstein's fingerprints, which eventually led to the arrest of Karpis in New Orleans. Unfortunately, she returned to the Woodcock House, upon Alvin's request, to retrieve the baby alligator he had bought in Hot Springs at the Arkansas Alligator Farm. (Above, courtesy of Fred Mark Palmer; right, courtesy of GCHS.)

Alvin Karpis, shown here in his favorite boater-style straw hat, was born in Montreal, Canada, in 1908. He moved to Topeka, Kansas, where he started a life of crime at an early age. Karpis received most of his education in prisons and jails, which is likely where he discovered his bisexuality. One of his partners, in more ways than one, was Fred Barker. Together with Harvey Bailey, Frank Nash, and Verne Miller, the Karpis-Barker Gang was known as a ruthless group of bank robbers. Their successful exploits attracted other professional criminals, and the gang grew in number. In 1932, Fred Barker invited his mother to join the boys on a sabbatical in Hot Springs. The gang enjoyed golf, gambling, and fishing with their wives and girlfriends. They had plenty of money in their pockets, and they were safe to move about Hot Springs, under the protection of the local police. (Courtesy of William J. Helmer.)

$1,200.00 REWARD $1,200.00

Twelve Hundred Dollars.

WANTED

For the Murder of C. R. Kelly, Sheriff of Howell County, Missouri, on December 19, 1931

ALVIN KARPIS

Gangsters of
Kimes-Inman
Gang of
Oklahoma
Missouri
Kansas and
Texas

FRED BARKER

DESCRIPTION: ALVIN KARPIS, alias George Dunn, alias R. E. Hamilton, alias Ray Karpis, alias Raymond Hadley, alias George Haller; Age 22; Height 5-9¾; Weight 130 lbs.; Hair-brown; Eyes-blue; Scars-cut SC base L. hand; Occupation, Worked in bakery.　　FPC　1-R-II-5
　　　　　　　　　　　　　　　　　1-U-UU-8
Karpis is ex-convict having served State Reformatory Hutchinson, Kansas, 1926, No. 7071　Also State Penitentiary Lansing, Kansas, May, 1930, Crime Burglary.

DESCRIPTION: FRED BARKER, alias F. G. Ward, alias Ted Murphy, alias J. Darrows; Age 28; Weight 120 lbs.; Height 5-4; Build-slim; Complexion-fair; Hair-sandy; Eyes-blue; Teeth-lower front gold, two upper front gold. Sentenced State Reformatory, Granite, Oklahoma. Robbery 1923. Sentenced State Penitentiary Lansing, Kan., March, 1927.
　　　　　　　　　　　　　FPC　29-I-20
　　　　　　　　　　　　　　　　20-O-22

　　These men acting together murdered Sheriff C. R. Kelly, West Plains, Missouri in cold blood when he attempted to arrest them.
　　The Chief of Police and Sheriff at West Plains, Missouri, will pay a reward of $300.00 each for the arrest and surrender of either of these men to Howell County, Missouri officers. $200.00 additional will be paid on conviction.　We will come after them any place.
　　An additional reward of $100.00 each will be paid for the arrest and surrender to Howell County officers of A. W. Dunlop and Old Lady Arrie Barker, Mother of Fred Barker. Dunlop is about 65 years of age; slender, white hair, full face Irishman. Mrs. Barker is about 60 years of age. All may be found together on farm. We hold Felony Warrants on all of these parties.
　　Police and other authorities: Keep this Poster before you at all times as we want these Fugitives. If further information is desired Wire Collect Chief of Police or Sheriff at West Plains, Missouri.

James A. Bridges
Chief of Police

Mrs. C. R. Kelly
Sheriff

West Plains, Missouri

JOURNAL PRINT, West Plains, Mo.

Alvin Karpis became Public Enemy No. 1, wanted for murder, bank robbery, train robbery, and kidnapping. J. Edgar Hoover and his men were always a few steps behind Karpis, until some of the former gang members were arrested and began to talk. Additionally, rewards for Karpis's capture, dead or alive, were producing leads to his whereabouts, and most pointed to Hot Springs. Karpis and his associate, Fred Barker, felt the heat and decided to leave Hot Springs. They headed south, narrowly escaping a raid on the Woodcock House. Time ran out for Alvin Karpis when he was apprehended by the FBI on May 22, 1936, in New Orleans. Sentenced to life imprisonment on Alcatraz, he joined many of his old gang members when he arrived there on August 7, 1936. The roster during Alvin's tenure at Alcatraz read like a who's who of American gangster history, and included Al Capone. When Alcatraz closed 25 years later, Karpis was transferred to McNeil Island Prison, from which he was later paroled. (Courtesy of William J. Helmer.)

In 1932, the Karpis-Barker Gang split up half a million dollars from their bank heists. In that year, the gang executed 17 bank robberies, averaging $74,300 per hit. As banks beefed up security to combat the crime wave in the Midwest, the gang found itself in more and more shootouts, and many guards and innocent bystanders would be killed in the crossfire. Alvin Karpis added kidnapping for ransom to his resume, as well as planning jobs for John Dillinger. Emboldened by public outcry, Congress broadened the power of the Justice Department, leading to the formation of the Federal Bureau of Investigation. Federal agents were mandated to carry firearms, and the Karpis-Barker Gang, along with their associates John Dillinger, Pretty Boy Floyd, Baby Face Nelson, Bonnie and Clyde, and a host of other notorious Hot Springs visitors, would have bull's-eyes on their backsides. (Courtesy of William J. Helmer.)

John Stover became the first manager of the Hot Springs Airport, in 1931. Stover facilitated regular flights between Little Rock and Hot Springs, set up a training school for pilots, and flew charter flights from what was commonly referred to as Stover Field. A couple of chartered flights led to problems for Stover. First, there was the flight of Frances Luce Nash and Dick Galatas to Joplin, Missouri, so that Nash could rendezvous with her recently arrested husband as he was being transported to Kansas City. The second was a chartered flight for Alvin Karpis and Grace Goldstein to attend the heavyweight fight between Joe Louis and Max Baer at Madison Square Garden in New York. The Karpis charter resulted in Stover's indictment for harboring a fugitive in 1938. Stover was found not guilty by Judge Thomas Trimble in US District Court in Little Rock. (Above, courtesy of Mary D. Hudgins Collection, Special Collections, University of Arkansas Libraries, Fayetteville; below, courtesy of Fred Mark Palmer.)

Visitors such as Charles Arthur Floyd (left) did not have to conceal their identities while in Hot Springs. The letter shown below is an example of the reports J. Edgar Hoover would receive regarding notorious Hot Springs figures. The contents of this letter are as follows: "Metropolis Ill, Mr. John Edgar Hoover, I have just heard from, or thru the (underworld) that Charles (Pretty Boy) Floyd has been seen lately and frequents Hot Springs ARK. and has been seen in conference with the Mayor, of that town, the Mayor having told him not to pull any rough stuff there and he would not be bothered. Floyd drives a large fine car with shatter proof glass, also he keeps all the glass up even in the summer time, also has a machine gun straped [sic] to him continuly [sic]. He is seen in Hot Springs about twice a month and stays 3 or 4 days at a time. Please answer my letter so I will know that your mail has not been tampered with. [signed,] James L Gordon, Metropolis Ill (Shoe Repair Shop)."

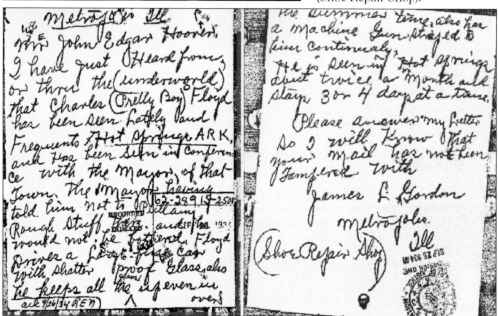

There weren't many places in America where the crime couple Bonnie Parker and Clyde Barrow could hide on their way to infamy, but Hot Springs, Arkansas, offered them more opportunity to relax than most places. Despite being two of the most famous bank robbers in history, Parker and Barrow were perhaps the poorest. According to family historian Buddy Barrow Williams, the two never came away from a bank robbery with more than $1,500. They spent most of their time robbing gas stations for fuel and small change. When Williams was asked the make of Clyde's favorite car, he replied, "The last one he stole." (Courtesy of Argenta Images.)

Shown here receiving a check from a local merchant, Hot Springs chief of detectives Herbert "Dutch" Akers (left) and chief of police Joe Wakelin (right) had more going for them than just law enforcement. Wakelin once went to Mayor McLaughlin and asked for a raise for himself and Akers. McLaughlin pointed out to the chief that if they could not make a living with a gun and a badge, perhaps they should look for a new line of work. The two made the best of the mayor's "leaf of gold" and ran more bribery schemes and payoff scams out of the police department than did most of the dangerous visitors who hid out in the spa city. Their own luck ran out following the arrest of Alvin Karpis. There was little doubt that, after witnesses testified seeing Akers and Wakelin in the company of America's last Public Enemy No. 1, the two police officers were indeed harboring the fugitive. The two, along with Grace Goldstein and police information officer Cecil Brock, were found guilty in 1938 and served time. (Courtesy of Clay White.)

Four

THE UNLUCKY
APRIL FOOL'S DAY

The last week in March 1936 found the morning peaceful as usual in the Valley of the Vapors, recalled Ed Attwater, veteran bell captain at the Arlington Hotel. Attwater had met many gangsters in his duties as a young bellboy at the Arlington in the early 1930s, but one particular meeting made a lasting impression.

The Oaklawn Thoroughbred Race Track live meet was under way, and the town was packed with race fans. Little did anyone know or expect that one of the spa city's most notorious and regular visitors would be spending his last few days of freedom in America in the resort.

Salvatore Lucania, or Charles "Lucky" Luciano, was in residence at the Arlington Hotel with one of his many girlfriends, Gay Orlova, or "Gay All Over," as Luciano called her. He had rendezvoused with Orlova in Cleveland after fleeing his Waldorf apartment in New York City based on a tip from a Waldorf employee that two New York detectives were on their way up to the 29th floor to talk to him.

Meanwhile, in Hot Springs, the poster boys for bad cops, chief of police Joe Wakelin and chief of detectives Dutch Akers, had legitimately arrested a man wanted for burglary in the Big Apple and summoned a couple of New York detectives to Hot Springs to pick up the fugitive.

Luciano knew that the sanctuary Hot Springs offered would give him time to figure out what was going on in New York. He received regular reports from his underboss, Albert Anastasia. Luciano and his female companion enjoyed the horse races, the thermal baths, the company of Owney and Agnes Madden, and the nightlife that Hot Springs offered.

On April 1, 1936, Lucky Luciano left the Arlington Hotel, dressed to the nines, on his way to the racetrack. But Lucky had not always come to Hot Springs so impeccably dressed. Ed Attwater remembered the first time he met Luciano in his suite at the hotel. "Lucky and his boys were playing cards and there were a few guns laying around on the bed." After receiving his tip for delivering the morning newspaper, Attwater was caught smiling and was asked by Luciano to explain the source of his amusement. The bellboy replied that he noticed Lucky was wearing orange socks with a blue suit. Luciano, in appreciation of the fashion advice, sent Attwater with a few hundred dollars to a downtown men's store to purchase a new suit of clothes that the bellboy thought more appropriate for Hot Springs attire. Lucky would don the suit during many more visits to the spa city. His final visit to Hot Springs, and the events that occurred thereafter, revealed that Charlie Luciano was anything but lucky.

Before the races started for the day, Luciano ran into an old friend, local badged racketeer Dutch Akers, the chief of detectives. His decision to kill time by taking a stroll down Bathhouse Row would prove to be Luciano's last act of "killing." Ironically, as the two men walked and talked, they were spotted by New York detective John Brennan, who had come to Hot Springs to pick up the aforementioned New York burglar that Wakelin and Akers had arrested. The New York cop recognized Luciano and informed him that New York attorney general Thomas Dewey and the entire East Coast were looking for him and that he would appreciate Lucky's returning to New York with him. Luciano declined the invitation, telling Brennan to stay out of it. The detective informed Lucky that he would have to report that he had seen him or he would lose his badge. A few hours later, Luciano was detained by Garland County deputy sheriff Marion Anderson on the request of Brennan. Luciano was bonded out by W.S. Jacobs, owner of the Southern Club, at the request of Owney Madden, according to the *Arkansas Gazette* of April 2, 1936. During Lucky's brief time behind bars, he met Milton Attwater, who had been arrested for murder. Attwater was the father of the young bellboy that Luciano had befriended at the Arlington. Lucky's release put the state of Arkansas on the precipice of national scandal.

The rage that rained down from New York governor Thomas Dewey forced the governor of Arkansas, Marion Futrell, to order the re-arrest of Luciano. The legal wrangling that ensued brought the attention of the world on Hot Springs. Luciano's lawyer, Moses Polakoff, and Dewey's deputy prosecutor, Edward McLean, along with hundreds of reporters, raced to Hot Springs by plane, train, and automobile. Some of Hot Springs' brightest legal minds filed a local charge against Luciano in an effort to help fight extradition. Luciano was rearrested at the Arlington, but he was afforded special privileges, like regular visits from Gay Orlova and the use of a telephone to speak with his attorney. Luciano in return bought deli sandwiches for the entire jail population. According to Orval Allbritton, former investigative clerk for the FBI and noted author, Luciano was treated by the Hot Springs political machine of Ledgerwood and McLaughlin as if he were the town's man of the year. A few days later, under pressure from Governor Futrell and Arkansas attorney general Carl Bailey, Garland County was forced to capitulate and turn Luciano over to a squadron of state rangers who threatened to take him by force. Luciano's claim that the charge of compulsory prostitution against him was political was correct, but he probably never dreamt that it would be the ire of an Arkansas politician that would bring about his tribulation. Attorney General Bailey became the next governor of Arkansas, based in part on the publicity and praise he received from Thomas Dewey and his public scorn of the illegal activities in Hot Springs. Bailey said of the incident, "Every time a major criminal of this country wants an asylum, he heads for Hot Springs. The publicity they complain about is going to warn criminals against blandishments from Hot Springs that they can come there and receive protection with their filthy lucre. Justice denied is justice delayed, and the state has within its borders a Number 1 criminal of the United States."

Dewey's request for Luciano's extradition took days to be granted. At midnight on April 16, while Luciano's attorney was on his way back from a Kansas City appeals court hearing about the matter, an overlooked deadline expired, and Charles "Lucky" Luciano was turned over to the deputy prosecuting attorney of New York, Edward McLean, and a team of New York police officers.

Charles Luciano ascended to the top of the largest crime family in New York by taking advantage of the war between his boss, Joe Masseria, and fellow Sicilian Salvatore Maranzano. Historians believe that Luciano got the nickname "Lucky" by surviving a bad beating, surviving a throat slashing, or because of the "Americanizing" of his surname. Masseria and Maranzano shared the fact that they were not equal-opportunity employers, but, rather, chose to hire only Sicilians. Luciano was admonished by Masseria for having friends, such as Costello, Lansky, and Madden, who fell outside of this edict. Luciano took the first step to the top when Ben Siegel, Joe Adonis, Albert Anastasia, and Vito Genovese assassinated Masseria at a Coney Island restaurant after Lucky excused himself from the table to use the men's room. This assured him the second position in the Maranzano outfit. Maranzano later suffered a fate similar to Masseria's, and Charles "Lucky" Luciano became the father of modern organized crime in the United States. (Courtesy of Corbis Images.)

When Galina Orlova came to America at the age of 16, it did not take long for her beauty to be noticed, and she was soon working on Broadway. Others besides theater producers, however, noticed Orlova's assets. She began to draw the attention of the underworld. Working in a show in Palm Island, Florida, Orlova met a dark-complexioned, handsome man whom she found to be conservative and quiet. That man was Charles "Lucky" Luciano, and she was smitten. One of the last times she was able to spend quality time with Lucky was on his ill-fated trip to Hot Springs in 1936, when he was arrested. She publicly voiced her objections to his arrest on prostitution charges. According to her, "Charlie" was "just like any other fellow. He was nice." (Courtesy of Argenta Images.)

One of the reasons Lucky Luciano (left) was considered by J. Edgar Hoover to be "the single man who organized crime in America" was that Luciano was able to bring men of different ethnic backgrounds into his circle. An example of this is his association with Meyer Lansky (right). From a very early age, Luciano respected Lansky's toughness; Lansky felt his organizational skills could be an asset to Lucky, and they were. Meyer Lansky II recalled that his grandfather "loved Hot Springs, Arkansas. He loved to patronize it as a tourist as well as a businessman. Prior to Las Vegas, Nevada, that was where everybody went to enjoy the hot springs, to enjoy each other, to work with the locals, to create business—everything they did there was good, and it brought the town a lot of prosperity at the time." (Courtesy of Historical Attractions Inc.)

	Number of Lockups	Amount			NAME	Sex	Color	When Committed			By What Authority Committed	For What Offense and For What Term	Date of Leaving Prison			Escaped or Discharged —If Discharged By What Authority	
								Mo.	Day	Yr.			Mo.	Day	Yr.		
					Harry Rosenberg	M	W	12	7	35	GJ	Embezzlement				Jail	
					Wm Houston	M	C	1	13	36	GJ	Gr. Larceny				Jail	
					Cecil James	M	C	1	13	36	GJ	Gr. Larceny				Jail	
					A. E. Morgan	M	W	1	24	36	GJ	Embezzlement	4	10	36	Tucker Farm 4 yr	
					Alton Windham	M	W	1	27	36	GJ	Gr. Larceny	4	6	36	Rel Houston Emey	
					Wm Malone	M	C	2	3	36	GJ	Built to Sell				Jail	
					C. C. Robbins	M	W	2	3	36	GJ	Gr. Larceny	4	16	36	Long Sug Witts	
					Buster Hancock	M	W	3	14	36	M.C.	Robbing	4	30	36	To M.C.	
1					Theo Holt	M	C	3	16	36	M.C.	Robbing	4	30	36	To M.C.	
2					Milton Attwater	M	C	3	24	36	M.C.	Murder	4	4	36	Bond	
3					Andrew Hudson	M	C	3	26	36	GJ	Robbing				Jail	
3					W. B. Berans	M	W	3	26	36	Montgomery Co	Murder	4	11	36	Ret to Mtg Co	
3					Chas Luciano	M	W	4	1	36	New York		4	4	36	Rel to State Rangers	
2			16		Eugene McKenzie	M	W	4	2	36	M.C.	D.I.L.	4	3	36	To M.C.	
6					Chas Wilder	M	W	4	4	36	M.C.	Liquor	4	4	36	appl Bond	
3					Clarence King	M	C	4	4	36	M.C.	Liquor	4	4	36	appl Bond	
1					Mrs Edna Russell	F	W	4	4	36	M.C.	Liquor				Jail	
1					Mrs Z.L. Menzel	F	W	4	4	36	M.C.	Liquor	4	7	36	appl issued	
4					Angie McKechnie	M	W	4	4	36	M.C.	D.I.L.	4	5	36	Bond	
4					Rex Brewerton	M	C	4	8	36	M.C.	Liquor	4	8	36	appl Bond	
7					Marion Carter	M	W	4	8	36			4	8	36		
1					Frank Andrews	M	W	4	3	36	Gulpha	Murder Ret	4	9	36	Rel to Leu	
1					Arthur Burrough	M	W	4	8	36	M.C.	D & D	4	9	36	Rel Earl Witt	
1					Jarrett Ingram	M	W	4	11	36	M.C.	Fake Pharm	4	11	36	Bond	
1					W. B. Berans	M	W	4	13	36	Montgomeryslo	Murder	4	25	36	Ret to Mongr Co.	
					Theo Meredith	M	W	4	14	36	M.C.	Larceny				Jail	

Veteran bell captain of the Arlington Resort Hotel, Ed Attwater, recalls Lucky Luciano bringing him news of his father's incarceration. Milton Attwater, Ed's father, is listed as the 10th entry on this Garland County Jail register of prisoners. Ironically, Luciano is registered as the 13th entry. When Luciano was released and returned to the Arlington Hotel, he saw Attwater and told him, "Your father is probably going to do time, but he said not to worry." Luciano assured Attwater that "everything would be okay, after all, it's just a matter of time." Attwater recalled one of the extra favors he did for Luciano: "I delivered flowers from 'Mr. Looziana' every morning to a lady in the hotel." When asked by other bellboys if he was catering to a gangster, he replied, "They're just like me and you, they just don't take no crap." (Courtesy of Historical Attractions Inc.)

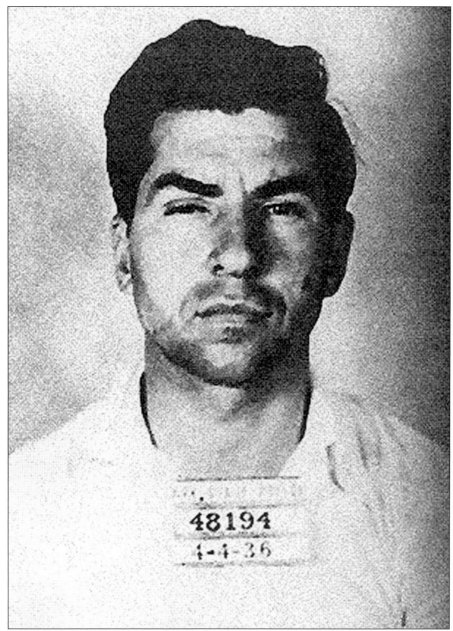

On June 18, 1936, Luciano was sentenced to 30 to 50 years at the maximum-security Dannemora Prison in New York. It was the longest sentence ever handed down in New York for compulsory prostitution. He served his time quietly, determined to be a model prisoner. During World War II, Luciano helped the government by forging ties and collecting intelligence in Sicily prior to the Allied invasion of Italy. In 1946, his sentence was commuted, and Luciano was deported to Italy, as he had never become an American citizen. The US government blocked his attempts to return to the Americas, including Cuba, and he lived the rest of his days in Italy. While he had several long-term mistresses in the United States and Italy, he never married and claimed no children. Luciano died of a heart attack on January 26, 1962, at Capodichino Airport in Naples, Italy, where he had gone to meet a Hollywood movie producer. (Courtesy of Historical Attractions Inc.)

Ben Siegel (shown here at left with George Raft), like his Jewish partner, Meyer Lansky, enjoyed spending time in the Springs. They began coming to the city with Costello and Luciano to play golf and tennis and ride horses, which were all part of the Arlington Hotel experience. While there might have been eyebrows raised in New York at seeing Italians and Jews together, there was no such prejudice in Hot Springs. (Courtesy of GCHS.)

Owney Madden, a former Harlem nightclub owner, never thought twice about entertaining black people in the deep South. Madden made friends from all walks of life. Some of his friends surprised him with gifts, like this Chris Craft runabout, given to him by actor George Raft. Owney had facilitated Raft's journey from a meager beginning in Hell's Kitchen to a major film star in Hollywood. (Courtesy of GCHS.)

William "Bill" Young (left, with Bob Murray, his assistant) was the hotel detective for the Arlington Hotel in the 1920s and 1930s. Young's job had many facets, but one in particular brought him face to face with one of the most famous Jewish mobsters in America. While patrolling the lobby, according to James "Ev" Young, Bill's son, his father spotted an attractive, well-dressed woman entering the hotel's revolving doors. Under the assumption that she was a "working girl," he intercepted the temptress and asked her to leave. Later, he was confronted by Benjamin "Bugsy" Siegel, who informed him that the woman he had thrown out of the hotel was no prostitute but his gal, Virginia Hill, and that if he insulted her again he would throw him off the roof of the hotel. Bill Young replied with assurance that Siegel would accompany him on the ride down. Moments later, Siegel began laughing, and the two became friends. (Courtesy of Jimmy Young.)

James Evelyn Young (right), son of Bill Young, Arlington Hotel detective, poses with his cousin, Garland County sheriff Elza Young. James Young had rich memories of growing up in Hot Springs. As a youngster, he caddied at Hot Springs Country Club and recalled other caddies joking about carrying the bag for Big Al Capone. Most of the time, Capone had one of his own men, wearing a fedora and carrying what appeared to be an empty golf bag, trailing the group. This fellow was identified as Eugene "Golf Bag" Hunt, and the bag was not completely empty—it held a Thompson machine gun. The caddies surmised that some of the fairways were open to view from the road and a little too accessible for the Chicago mobster's security. Later in life, Young was a successful bookie and club owner. He especially loved operating a floating craps game. Young, a close friend of Owney Madden, said, "Owney gave me the horsebook for $50 a week, and all the bigger joints were paying $200 a week. Owney had an 'in' with Mr. Marcello, and that was good for all of us." (Courtesy of Jimmy Young.)

Five

THE ONLY MAN
EXILED IN AMERICA

Hot Springs was a diamond in the rough in 1931. William S. Jacobs controlled the gambling, Leo McLaughlin was beginning to grease the gears of his political machine, and municipal judge Verne Ledgerwood was trying to balance the illegal activities of the spa city with the factions opposed to the wide-open gambling, prostitution, and curbside drunks. This dysfunction must have been enticing to Owen Madden and Dutch Schultz when they stopped over in Hot Springs on their way to consult Gov. Huey P. Long concerning his own gambling empire in Louisiana. Madden had spent nine years in Sing Sing for his role in the murder of rival gang member Patsy Doyle. A condition of his release, set forth by New York attorney general Thomas Dewey, was that he would no longer be allowed to return to New York City. In essence, he was exiled as part of his parole agreement. He later served a few months in prison for violating this ruling. Upon his release, Madden moved to Hot Springs for good. He sold his Manhattan brewery, the Phoenix Cereal Beverage Company, to Maj. Thomas G. Lanphier of Bird Aircraft Corp. Not only was the construction of a plane for Madden part of the deal, but so were flying instructions from Lanphier, according to a *Time* magazine article of June 26, 1933. Lanphier was a business partner with Charles Lindbergh, famous for piloting the *Spirit of St. Louis*.

Madden divested himself of his New York interests, including his ownership of the famous Cotton Club and Stork Club. He retained his shares in Tropical Park and Hialeah Thoroughbred Racetracks in Florida with Meyer Lansky. Madden settled quietly into Hot Springs and began polishing the "diamond city" like a New York jeweler.

Madden wove his way into the fabric of Hot Springs almost seamlessly. He would get his hair cut every Friday at the barbershop in the lower level of the Arlington Hotel, visit the Southern Club, take a bath at the Superior bathhouse virtually every day, and spend time with his attorney and close ally, Q. Byrum Hurst Sr.

Madden's life in New York had not been as predictable, even in the early days. After being in America for only a short time, he became a member of the Gopher Gang. His role was limited to petty theft, extortion, and protection. He soon graduated, however, to grand larceny and, eventually, murder. Hot Springs offered him a much different life.

Madden's life began in Leeds, England, in 1891. He enjoyed a fairly normal childhood until a policeman stepped on a rock on the edge of a hill. The resulting rockslide destroyed one of Madden's dovecotes, or pigeon coops, and killed some of his pigeons. Although it was an accident, the young Owen Madden never accepted that, and he languished in despair. This incident left him with a deep hatred of the police that he would carry into his new life in America. After his father died, Madden's mother went to America to help her sister, who had moved to New York. She left the children in an orphanage in Leeds. A year later, she booked passage for them, and Owney, his older brother Martin, and his younger sister Mary, boarded the SS *Teutonic* and sailed to New York City. Owen's disdain for authority and his reputation as a fierce fighter made him a prominent member and, eventually, the leader of the Gopher Gang. His prowess in the protection rackets gained him favor with New York politicians, who used Madden and his boys to assure that the voters standing in line at the polls would cast their ballots in the right direction. Madden had been shot many times and refused to enlist the services of the police. Each time he returned to the streets after his recovery, fear of him grew among rival gangs. As Madden climbed the gangland ladder, he acquired the nickname "The Killer" for his propensity to knock off those who did him harm or got in his way.

People in Hot Springs found it hard to believe that the quiet, gentle Englishman had killed six or seven men and was New York's most notorious gangster. And they never suspected that he wore a specially made corset that held his intestines in place, the result of injuries suffered in a machine-gun ambush. Madden fell in love with and married Agnes Demby, whom he had met and dined with during an earlier visit to the spa city. But his faithfulness to her was dubious. At least one woman claimed Madden fathered her child, and several others boasted of relationships with the blue-eyed New Yorker in the white cap. His alleged forays crossed racial boundaries. Agnes, a shopkeeper and the daughter of the Hot Springs postmaster, was aware that Madden was no choirboy. In fact, Madden had introduced Agnes to one of his former lovers in New York, Mae West.

Madden brought with him to Hot Springs a small fortune, which garnered him respect in some circles, but especially that of Mayor Leo P. McLaughlin. Madden became the architect for the way things would work best in Hot Springs. His plan was that the gamblers as well as the rest of the community would benefit. His mostly anonymous philanthropy would build the largest boys' club in the state at that time, and he was known to have purchased new uniforms for the Hot Springs High School band, of which William J. Clinton would one day be a member. Madden's close association with New York and Chicago Mafia legends, who regularly visited him in Hot Springs, left J. Edgar Hoover suspicious and always questioning Madden's retirement lifestyle. Fearing deportation in 1942, Madden applied for US citizenship. He was armed with a list of his charitable contributions; a good reference from a close friend of the judge, Garland County sheriff Marion Anderson; and an ally in Washington whom the Maddens had supported financially in his bid for the US Senate, John McClellan. Owen Vincent Madden was granted citizenship on March 16, 1942, after pledging allegiance to the United States of America.

Owney Madden (second row, fourth from left) is pictured here with his gang, the Gophers. He had two things going for him when he arrived on Ellis Island as a kid and moved to Hell's Kitchen, the roughest neighborhood in New York City: he loved pigeons, and he hated cops. These were qualities shared by his playmates. Madden also had all the qualities of a strong leader, and carried them with him all through his life. By all accounts, Madden had what it took to be a boss, and knew what he had to do to maintain a following. He was ambitious, cocky, generous to his men, ruthless to his enemies, and never in his life broke his word to anyone. Even as a young boy, Madden was fearless. He would taunt overweight cops to get them to chase him around corners, over fences, and down hallways. If and when they caught him, they would beat him unconscious. He never complained. He just woke up and went back to work as the head of the Gopher Gang. (Courtesy of Fred Mark Palmer.)

Madden began serving time in Sing Sing for his role in the killing of Little Patsy Doyle in 1915. Within two years, he had organized prizefights and baseball games and had become the right-hand man of the warden, Lewis Laws. Warden Laws and Madden became good friends, and Madden was afforded privileges that even the guards weren't allowed. According to one New York newspaper reporter, Madden wore silk shirts and smoked cigars in Sing Sing. He was released on good behavior in 1923. He returned to a different world than the one he had left, but the political connections he had established would aid in his reintegration into the Big Apple. Ever resourceful, Madden adapted. He began highjacking liquor trucks, and the company that owned the trucks eventually offered him an interest in the business. He parlayed that into ownership of a brewery, nightclubs, laundries, and thoroughbred racetracks, and the management of prizefighters. (Courtesy of GCHS.)

Originally opened as Club De Luxe in 1920 by heavyweight boxing champion Jack Johnson, the famous Harlem nightclub was renamed the Cotton Club when it was taken over by Owney Madden and "Big Frenchy" De Mange in 1923. The cover of the club's menu is pictured here. In keeping with the theme of the club's namesake, the black employees were dressed as plantation workers or in jungle attire. Performers such as Fletcher Henderson, Duke Ellington, and Cab Calloway honed their craft during their tenures at the club. It was mostly patronized by white clientele in the Prohibition era, and Madden was able to sell his "No. 1 Beer" (produced from Madden's Phoenix Cereal Beverage Company) with little intervention from the law. The club was shut down on several occasions during this time, but it was able to quickly reopen its doors because of Madden's political connections. (Courtesy of Historical Attractions Inc.)

Seen here with Max Baer (left) and Jack Dempsey, Primo Carnera (right) was the heavyweight champion of the world in 1933. However, he is most known for his connection with the mob, in particular, Owney Madden. Carnera may have been the largest heavyweight in history, but he was no match against the skills of a ruthless little mobster like Madden. Most historians believe Madden fixed all or most of Carnera's fights. Paul Gallico, a respected New York sportswriter, was an eyewitness to Carnera's rise and fall. He wrote in 1947, "there is probably no more scandalous, pitiful, incredible story in all the record of these last mad sports years than the tale of the living giant, a creature out of the legends of antiquity, who was made into a prize fighter." (Courtesy of the Fred Mark Palmer Collection.)

Details of Madden's release from Sing Sing appeared in a June 6, 1933, article in the *New York Times* that read in part: "Owen Madden will leave Sing Sing prison July 1 on parole after having served five days less than a year for violation of a previous parole. In underworld parlance Madden is a 'big-shot' racketeer with a finger in bootleg beer, running nightclubs, prizefighting, laundry racketeering and various illicit enterprises; in the records of the Parole Board he is a convict who was released on parole in 1933 after a single conviction. He served eight years of a sentence of from ten to twenty years for manslaughter and was recommitted in 1932 for violation of parole. . . . During the last year Madden spent his time at work in the green houses and the prison garden. Inside the stone walls he kept to himself and took no part in recreational activities, not even as a spectator at the entertainments and athletic events." Madden, a multimillionaire, had violated his parole by not being employed, a condition of his earlier release. His next move was to Hot Springs. (Courtesy of Corbis Images.)

On December 3, 1935, Owen Madden, 43, and Agnes Demby, 34 (above), were married at the Demby home at 506 West Grand in Hot Springs (below). Madden settled into Hot Springs life with his wife and father-in-law, with whom they lived until 1947, when James Demby died. That year, Owney and Agnes completely remodeled the home, sparing no expense. Madden continued to enjoy his pigeons, kept in a coop in the backyard, and Agnes raised chickens. They had many pets, including a large talking parrot named Prince. The bird was known to mimic Madden, using his favorite curse, "son of a bitch," at very inopportune times, according to family members. (Above, courtesy of GCHS; below, Mark Palmer Collection.)

In the 1930s, the celebrity status of Mayor Leo McLaughlin was a politician's best friend. US senator Huey Pierce Long, former Louisiana governor, seen in the photograph at right with his wife, Rose McConnell Long, celebrated a vacation at the Arlington Hotel in 1932. At that time, McLaughlin (above, left) presented Senator Long with a key to the city, a symbol of McLaughlin's approval that would ensure Long's top-drawer status in Hot Springs. Unfortunately, not everyone back in Louisiana respected Long's Hot Springs connections. He was assassinated three years later, in September 1935, in Baton Rouge. In Louisiana, the wealthy rejoiced and the poor mourned his demise. His wife would go on to finish his term in the US Senate, becoming Louisiana's first female senator, supported in part by New Orleans crime boss Carlos Marcello. (Above, courtesy of Historical Attractions Inc.; right, courtesy of Argenta Images.)

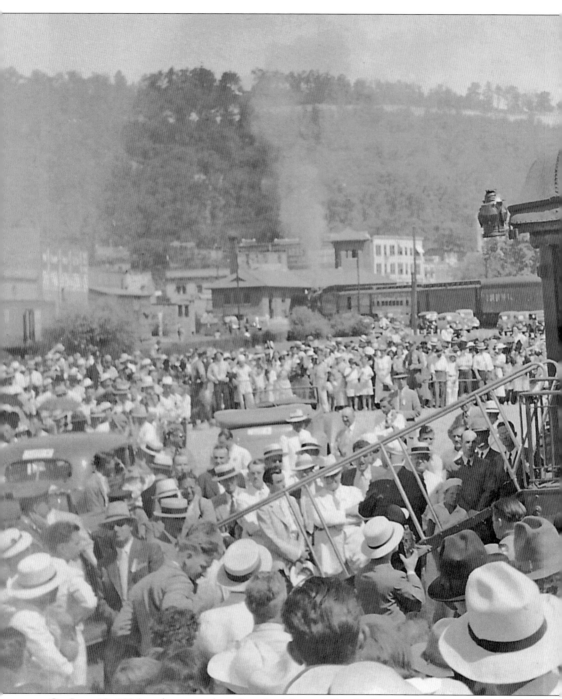

On June 10, 1936, a throng gathered at the Missouri Pacific depot to see the president of the United States arrive in Hot Springs. Standing on the platform are, from left to right, Gov. Marion Futrell, Pres. Franklin Roosevelt, Sen. Joseph T. Robinson, Mayor Leo P. McLaughlin, Harvey Couch, the founder of Arkansas Power and Light Company, and a team of Secret Service agents.

Harvey Couch entertained the dignitaries at his palatial estate, Couchwood, before the group traveled to Rockport and then on to Little Rock. The group was in the state to celebrate the Arkansas centennial. (Courtesy of GCHS.)

The mayor of New York City, Jimmie Walker (left), receives Mayor Leo McLaughlin's token of approval by being presented with the key to the city on the steps of the Arlington Hotel. Historians say that McLaughlin so admired Walker's lifestyle that he used it as a model for his own political persona. (Courtesy of Special Collections, University of Fayetteville, Mary Hudgins Collection.)

Always the showman, Leo McLaughlin, shown here with light heavyweight champion Billy Conn (right), would parade on Central Avenue every evening with his horses, Scotch and Soda. McLaughlin's team of horses was a symbol of his popularity in the city. His dapper dress and good looks, along with his silver tongue, endeared him to the voters. (Courtesy of Historical Attractions Inc.)

Mickey Cohen is seen here with his stripper girlfriend, Candy Bar. In his autobiography, *In My Own Words*, Cohen tells of Costello and Anastasia pulling a prank on Owney Madden: "They once pulled a rib on Owney Madden. When he was in Hot Springs, Arkansas, they picked up an old barrel of a broad on the streets, not a prostitute, but a real derelict woman and they sent her up where Owney Madden was at the Arlington Hotel. Now the top mahoffs from all over the country were sitting there with Mr. Madden, and it was all very proper. So this old barrel busts into this big meeting and said, 'Where's my sweetheart, Owney Madden?'" Cohen recalled one of his own Arlington experiences: "It just happened to be that Muscle Tony was there, one of the guys from Cleveland. Tony and his wife came down and had an Italian dinner at the hotel—it was something, that dinner. See there were some people there that still remembered me from my heydays, even though so many years passed. One of the managers of the hotel still remembered me. So the chef and he fixed this here Italian dinner for me. Well, God, you never seen anything like it! It was ridiculous." (Courtesy of Argenta Images.)

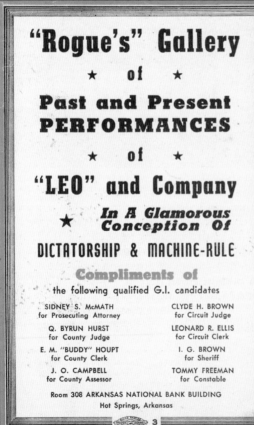

The 1946 political cartoon above was part of a campaign brochure the GI movement published to expose the scope of Mayor Leo McLaughlin's power. Norwood Phillips, a prominent attorney, son of a club owner, and nephew of McLaughlin, said, "There were enough ballots in the ballot box before the polls opened to elect his slate of candidates, so he had no problems there. Leo used to take a box of hundred dollar bills to my dad and have them exchanged for thousand dollar bills. My dad told him he should stop that because an FBI man told him they were watching him, and he did." The general consensus around the city was that, if you ran against McLaughlin, he was your enemy—and that meant you had an enemy for life. (Courtesy of Historical Attractions Inc.)

No story sums up the GI Revolt better than this extract of an article written by the columnist and author Spider Rowland: "For some 25 years Mayor Leo McLaughlin has been political potentate of Hot Springs and Garland County. Not only that, but in some state politics he drew more water than the Queen Mary. McLaughlin had more tricks up his sleeve than a puzzle factory. Nobody in the state with half-sense and one eye gave McMath's team any more chance than a milk cow in the Kentucky Derby." Rowland would live long enough to see the McLaughlin machine overthrown; however, the old boss was replaced by a new set of bosses, and life went on, wide open, under the watchful eye of Owney Madden. Shown here are, from left to right, (seated) Clyde H. Brown, circuit judge; Sid McMath, prosecuting attorney; and I.G. Brown, sheriff; (standing) Leonard R. Ellis, circuit clerk; Ray Owen, tax collector; E.M. Houpt, county clerk; J.O. Campbell, tax assessor; Q. Byrum Hurst, county judge; and Billy Joe Wilkerson, county treasurer. (Courtesy of Q. Byrum Hurst Jr.)

The mantle of Leo McLaughlin's political power would be assumed by a new group of men. After two years of trying to operate without gambling (following the GI revolt), the city's politicians realized that gambling might have been what was keeping Hot Springs afloat. This opened an old wound from the McLaughlin era and led to political cartoons, such as the one shown here, that appeared in the local newspaper, *The Sentinel-Record*. There was no mystery about who was in control. Although the members of the choir may have changed, the song remained the same. (Courtesy of Jimmy Young.)

Sidney Sanders McMath (1912–2003) was the 34th governor of Arkansas (1949–1953). No one gave Sid McMath a snowball's chance in hell of winning his bid for Garland County prosecuting attorney in 1946 against the powerful McLaughlin political regime. But McMath felt that, compared to commanding a regiment in the Pacific theater during World War II, fighting to give back control of his hometown to the people was not such a daunting task. Armed with a law degree from the University of Arkansas that he received before the war and aided by some good luck, McMath won the election. Some disabled phone lines to the county polling sites prohibited McLaughlin from knowing how many votes he needed to create to defeat McMath. Soon McMath's GI brethren would win other local elections, and the end of Leo McLaughlin was in sight, allowing McMath to pursue loftier goals. He recalled that, while he was prosecuting attorney in Hot Springs, he was summoned to the street one night by someone in a large black vehicle. He strolled down his long driveway to find the rear passenger window of the car being rolled down, and there he met Owen Vincent Madden for the first time. Madden congratulated him on his victory and said there were a couple of fellows in the Garland County Jail that, if released, Madden would guarantee their exodus from the city. McMath said he would have to think about it and returned to his home. As McMath walked up his driveway, he recalled hearing the car engine idling and wondering why the car was not pulling away. He remarked that this was the longest walk of his life. The next day, McMath contacted Madden and stated that he could not release the men. Madden thanked him for his consideration, and nothing else was ever said.

HURST

In 1941, Q. Byrum Hurst was licensed to practice law in Arkansas at the age of 23, making him the youngest person to become an attorney in the state at that time. After his tour of duty in the US Army, he returned to Hot Springs and was elected Garland County judge in 1947. He was part of the GI movement that overthrew McLaughlin's political machine. In 1950, he was elected to the Arkansas state Senate. His friendship with Owney Madden would prove to be helpful in a tax evasion charge that was brought against him by the government in 1963. Hurst had represented Jimmy Hoffa in an earlier trial, and this led Bobby Kennedy to cast a disparaging eye on Hurst and the well-publicized activities in the spa city. Madden would testify in the 1963 grand jury hearing that Hurst borrowed $20,000 from him and never repaid it. This significantly lowered Hurst's net income for the year in question, and Hurst was off the hook. (Courtesy of Q. Byrum Hurst Jr.)

The Ritter Hotel, at 217 Exchange Street, served as Owney Madden's office and the headquarters of the Downtown Printing Company, which in reality was the location of Madden's horse book, or wire service. Its location (near the central office of the local telephone company) insured that Madden would have racing results from around the country before anyone else. Wires were strung down Exchange Street and the base of West Mountain to at least eight bookie joints on Central Avenue. Madden originally got his information from New York sources, but he transferred his business to Carlos Marcello in New Orleans after the attempted assassination of his friend Frank Costello by Vincent "the Chin" Gigante. The Ritter was owned by Q. Byrum Hurst Sr., one of Madden's local attorneys. Madden sold his wire service and retired in the late 1950s after new federal regulations were introduced by Robert Kennedy concerning interstate commerce, including the use of telephones and telegraph. (Courtesy of GCHS.)

Owen Madden brought with him from New York a reputation for being a murderer, convict, mobster, and racketeer, but his life in Hot Springs was the antithesis of his past. Madden, shown holding Agnes's cousin Joe Demby, was a friend to all children and the down-and-out in the spa city. He had even begun to like some cops, especially his next-door neighbor, Hot Springs police chief John Ermey. Madden once offered a young patrolman a handful of cash to buy his family a new car after overhearing the officer's woes about his old, disabled vehicle. The young patrolman scoffed at the idea and told Madden he was not that kind of cop. Madden would not take "no" for an answer. The next day, Christmas Eve, the patrolman received a box from Clyde's men's store. When opened, the box contained a man's full-length fur coat with a $100 bill in each pocket and no clue as to the identity of the sender. The patrolman attempted to return the gift to the store, to no avail. Clyde would keep Santa's secret. (Courtesy of Joe Demby.)

Owney, seen at left in the photograph to the right with an unidentified couple, enjoyed the retired life Hot Springs afforded. His friends from New York, Chicago, Miami, and New Orleans could visit him regularly, play a little golf, enjoy some fine dining, play the horses, and take hot baths. Many believed that Madden still played a role in the underworld by conveying messages, stories, and decisions among the different bosses. If there was one thing that everyone knew, Madden, whether a mafia boss or the paperboy, kept his word, and he could be trusted by everyone. In his later years, he could be spotted walking down the street dressed in white, wearing a smile that could knock a person down. He was a man of slight build with a falcon-like nose. His piercing blue eyes darted about, watching everything around him that moved. (Courtesy of Fred Mark Palmer.)

In the below photograph, Leonard R. Ellis Jr. (left), sheriff of Garland County from 1955 to 1960, poses with his deputies. He expanded the role of the sheriff's department in the community, being the first to outfit his department with uniforms, creating the first mounted patrol, putting the first sheriff's boat on the lake, and starting the junior deputy program. In 1959, Sheriff Ellis said about Hot Springs, "We have kept gambling a local affair. All operators of gambling are local people. Over the years, outsiders occasionally try to get in. The business people of this community over a period of years have had a closed and sometimes an open town. It is a proven fact that when the town is open business is better. Because of the way we are situated, we have no business or industry. All of our business comes from visitors." (Left, courtesy of Garland County Sheriff's Department; below, courtesy of Historical Attractions Inc.)

The only thing that could bring together the two opposing sides of the gambling issue in Hot Springs was a parade. Both gamblers and reformists came out to support the veterans on Memorial Day. The tank rolling down Central Avenue in the above photograph is passing in front of St. Mary's of the Springs Catholic Church. One local patriot, not an American citizen at the time of the war, did what he could to help the cause. When a uniformed serviceman came to have lunch at the Southern Grill, Owney Madden, who was there most days, anonymously paid the tab. (Courtesy of Mary D. Hudgins Collection, Special Collections, University of Arkansas Libraries, Fayetteville.)

Although Hot Springs was located in what many would consider a remote area, millions of people visited the spa city to gamble. Gangsters, wealthy oilmen, tycoons, and even some locals would come into the city and try to match wits against road gambling legends such as Nick "the Greek" Dandolas, Amarillo Slim, Murph Harrold, and Benny Binion, to name just a few. To put it simply, Hot Springs was Las Vegas before Las Vegas had water, and the illegal gambling was so wide open that most Arkansans grew up thinking it was legal. The Southern Club (left) and the Belvedere (below) were two of the hottest spots. (Courtesy of Historical Attractions Inc.)

Although gambling was illegal, many newspapers around the country inadvertently advertised the spa city by reporting on its activities. One such example appeared in *The St. Louis Post-Dispatch* on March 29, 1959: "The Southern is the largest casino within the city limits and the oldest gambling establishment here. Its two-story structure nestles against West Mountain, part of which was carved out for the casino's expansion. On the first floor is the restaurant, which does a thriving business. Live lobsters from Maine and jumbo shrimp from New Orleans are flown in daily. The gambling casino on the second floor draws a crowd each night. Two men sit at the top of the wide marble stairway to the casino carefully scrutinizing visitors. They refuse admittance to undesirable patrons. The Southern's casino has five dice tables, three roulette wheels, four blackjack games, two chuck-a-luck cages, and sixteen slot machines. . . . There is a bar where alcoholic beverages are sold at modest prices. Sale of liquor by the drink is illegal under Arkansas law." (Courtesy of Tyler Seiz.)

MISCELLANEOUS
CITY OF HOT SPRINGS   No. 23655

NAME _Chum Inn_
ADDRESS _117 Walnut_

DATE PAID	DESCRIPTION	AMOUNT
MAR 2'67	2 28 .67	40.00 # 9+
Privilege		_bgm_ CITY CLERK

CITY OF HOT SPRINGS, ARKANSAS
OCCUPATION (AMUSEMENT) TAX STAMP
(This Is Not a License)

RECEIVED OF _Chum Inn_
117 Walnut

Classification	Amount	Tax Paid to
LARGE CASINO		
SMALL CASINO		
HANDBOOK		
RACING RESULTS		
BINGO		
SLOT MACHINES (4)	40°°	2-28-67
PINBALL MACHINES ( )		
BAR		

Date Paid ___ 3-2-67

EMMETT JACKSON
City Clerk

Nº   171

By ___ _bgm_

D. C

During the days of illegal gambling, over 100 businesses were charged an "amusement tax" by the City of Hot Springs. Slot machines were charged at a rate of $5 per month. The cost of operating bingo and card games was $50. Fees for small casinos and bars varied, depending, apparently, on the size of the operation. As seen in this document, The Chum Inn, at 117 Walnut Street, was charged double the monthly rate for slot machines. Names, addresses, and amounts were recorded on the city's ledger sheets. Noticeably missing from this ledger are some of the larger clubs, such as the Southern Club, the Arlington Hotel, the Vapors, and the Belvedere. One can only assume that these operations paid a blanket fee to license their illegal activities. (Courtesy of Historical Arkansas Productions Inc.)

If ever there were two guys strolling down the street looking like FBI men, it would be the men pictured at right. They are, in fact, a security team that worked for Owney Madden, and their job while in Hot Springs was to protect Rocky Marciano. Below is an authentic FBI man, Special Agent Leander "Lee" Muncy. In 1946, Muncy was assigned to Hot Springs. He rented a house on Grand Avenue. Little did he know that Owney Madden lived across the street. According to Lee Muncy Jr., "Mr. Madden always believed that J. Edgar Hoover had moved my dad into that house to keep an eye on him, but in fact it was the only house available at the time and my dad did not even know who Owney Madden was, much less where he lived." (Right, courtesy of Historical Attractions Inc.; below, courtesy of Lee Muncy Jr.)

Senior resident agent Clay White (left, with fellow agent Bob Hickam), was the eyes and ears of the FBI in Hot Springs from 1954 through 1977. In those years, he was charged with reporting on some of the most notorious criminals who visited the spa city. At the same time, he conducted local investigations, such as that of Maxine Harris Jones, the city's most visible and outspoken madam. Through the execution of his duty, White became acquainted with Owney Madden. Agent White related the circumstances surrounding Madden's first crime: "Owney said, 'Clay, I remember the first crime I ever committed, I was fifteen. I hit a man in the head with a stick of wood and he fell to the ground. I didn't want to kill him, I just wanted to knock him out. He fell to the ground, and I took his money. I think it was $500.' " Madden went on to tell White that he delivered the money to his aunt so that she could distribute it to his family without his mother's questioning its origin. (Courtesy of Clay White.)

Six

FRANK COSTELLO MAKES HIS MARK

If ever a man could put a new face on the Mafia, that man would surely be Frank Costello. Born Francesco Castiglia in Calabria, Italy, in 1891, he came to America with his parents in search of a better life. His young life in East Harlem, New York, however, would be anything but better. Employment for his parents was hard to come by, and young Francesco wound up in the rackets, into which many boys around Hell's Kitchen were drawn at that time. Like most of the mob bosses who preceded him, Castiglia worked his way up through the ranks, and the friends he made on his rise to power would be with him for the rest of his life, regardless of their ethnicity.

After serving time for being in possession of a firearm in 1913, he decided he would no longer be caught carrying a weapon; others, such as Albert Anastasia, his best friend from the neighborhood, would do that for him. With Anastasia as his enforcer, Francesco Castiglia, who changed his name to Frank Costello, ascended to the top of the New York mob almost by default. Lucky Luciano had been put away on a compulsory prostitution charge, and the families chose Costello as a new prime minister of the underworld. His peaceful people skills were like none other before him. He, like Luciano, was able to maintain the cooperation and support of other ethnic groups, such as the Bugs-Meyer Gang, comprised of its two famous Jewish leaders, Bugsy Siegel and Meyer Lansky; the English Godfather, Owen Madden; and most of the Sicilian families in New York. Frank Costello's interests, however, lay more in gambling and women than in being head of the Mafia. It was these desires that attracted him to Hot Springs. His knowledge and ownership of slot machine manufacturers became valuable assets to the blossoming Spa Amusement Company, created in Hot Springs to produce slots. His personality, flamboyance, and political connections made him very popular in the spa city, even before he became the high boss.

While a struggle ensued over who would control gambling in the resort town following the demise of W.S. Jacobs, an emissary was sent to Costello to inquire of his possible involvement in a solution to the problem. A group of casino owners felt that Costello would be the right man for the job. It was no secret that he had a financial interest in the Jack Tar Court hotel as well as in some of the other gambling establishments in the city. While staying at that hotel on Park Avenue, he was briefed on the details of his compensation package should he choose to become the new gambling czar. As Costello considered his options, word of his supposed interest leaked out and was published by the *Arkansas Democrat* on November 4, 1951. Just two days later, a special delivery airmail letter signed by Costello arrived at the offices of the *Hot Springs Sentinel-Record* that would lay to rest the "pipe dream," as circuit court judge C. Floyd Huff called it.

Huff would be one of those most affected by Costello's decision, as he had a stake in the illegal gambling operations.

The letter, which appeared on November 6, 1951, on the front page of *The Sentinel-Record* as a letter to the editor, read:

> My attention has been called to a rumor of a plan to make me "gambling czar" of Hot Springs.
>
> There is no truth whatsoever to this story. I never had the remotest idea of engaging in or being connected with the gambling business in Hot Springs or any other place in Arkansas—directly or indirectly.
>
> For over twenty-five years I have been a regular visitor of Hot Springs. Like countless thousands of others, I have found immense enjoyment and pleasure in its wonderful climate, its incomparable mineral baths and its hospitable people.
>
> Frank Costello

After a couple of "contract fulfillments" with federal prisons, Costello again would begin his vacations in the Spa. Agnes Madden recalled that Frank and Joe Adonis would take her to play golf at Hot Springs Country Club as far back as the 1930s, while Madden was serving his own sentence for parole violation. It was not unusual to see Frank Costello, Meyer Lansky, Jimmy "Blue Eyes" Allo, and Ralph Capone visiting Owney Madden and taking in all the amenities that Hot Springs had to offer.

Having stepped down as the head of the Mafia, and with a little "coaxing" from Vito Genovese's hit man Vincent "Chin" Gigante, Costello went into retirement, as had Owney Madden. He still loved gambling, which kept him coming to Hot Springs to visit Owney and Agnes for years to come. The two old viceroys of vice would spend many days of their rocking years on the veranda of the Arlington Hotel, talking about New York City the way it was and the way it could have been. They were joined occasionally by old friends from Chicago and New York, bringing news from the cities. But the two men were at a stage in their lives they had always hoped to reach. They had achieved something very few people in their profession or lifestyle had ever achieved. They were old, they were alive, they could still hit a golf ball, and they could still hold their own across the green felt of a poker table.

Frank Costello reluctantly took control of the New York crime syndicate upon the arrest and eventual deportation of Lucky Luciano. "Frank was not into shooting people," local historian Mark Palmer says. "He loved to gamble, and he loved the ladies." Costello enjoyed sitting across the table from some of the top road gamblers in the country when they worked their way through Hot Springs. In addition, he loved spending time with Owney Madden, who was an old New York chum from the neighborhood. Costello, with his friend Meyer Lansky, played golf, took the baths, and could be seen sitting on the veranda of the Arlington Hotel overlooking what he called "Manhattan in miniature." Through the years, Costello would have to battle not only the Internal Revenue Service but also the jealousy of Vitone Genovese over his default title, "Prime Minister of the Underworld." (Courtesy of Corbis Images.)

Although some historians question the role of the underworld in the ownership of Hot Springs' gambling empire, no one doubts the relationship between Frank Costello and Chef Alfred "Gee" Raso. Raso came to America with his parents, as Costello did, at the turn of the century, from Calabria, Italy. His path would be similar to that of his friend. Raso did odd jobs for the Capone outfit in Chicago at an early age. Unlike Costello, however, he had an interest in cooking and decided to join the Army. He served in France and would later joke to his restaurant customers about learning to cook in a French culinary school, according to his friend Mark Palmer. Gee's Villa Nova (below), located on 3900 Central Avenue, just south of Oaklawn Park Race Track, was a popular hangout for prizefighters, major-league baseball players, and prominent members of the Mafia. Costello had loaned Raso the money to build the Villa Nova and was quite comfortable with Gee's stewardship of his investment and, moreover, with Gee's honor. In the photograph at left, Raso (left) poses with Champ Segal. (Courtesy of Mark Palmer.)

In 1951, Albert Anastasia (above) was making plans to retire in the spa city. In an article that same year in the *Sentinel-Record*, he was referred to as the "lord high executioner of Murder, Inc." and "Brooklyn waterfront boss." Circuit Judge C. Floyd Huff Jr. said in the article, "We're not going to have him here. If he thinks he can run away from New York mobsters and run down here, he'd better think again. He can do his running in some other direction." Anastasia continued to visit Owney Madden in Hot Springs despite his plans to retire in the spa city being thwarted by local bosses. In October 1957, Madden and Chef Gee Raso reluctantly placed Anastasia on a plane at the Hot Springs Airport just days before he was slain in the Park Sheraton barbershop in Midtown Manhattan. (Courtesy of Historical Attractions Inc.)

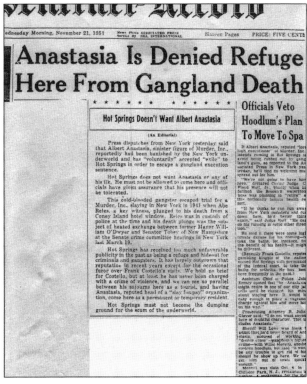

ednesday Morning, November 21, 1951   Sixteen Pages   PRICE: FIVE CENTS

Anastasia Is Denied Refuge Here From Gangland Death

Officials Veto Hoodlum's Plan To Move To Spa

Hot Springs Doesn't Want Albert Anastasia

(An Editorial)

Press dispatches from New York yesterday said that Albert Anastasia, sinister figure of Murder, Inc., reportedly had been banished by the New York underworld and has "voluntarily" accepted "exile" to Hot Springs in order to escape a gangland execution sentence.

Hot Springs does not want Anastasia or any of his ilk. He must not be allowed to come here and officials have given assurance that his presence will not be tolerated.

This cold-blooded gangster escaped trial for a Murder, Inc., slaying in New York in 1941 when Abe Reles, a key witness, plunged to his death from a Coney Island hotel window. Reles was in custody of police at the time and his death plunge was the subject of heated exchange between former Mayor William O'Dwyer and Senator Tobey of New Hampshire at the Senate crime committee hearings in New York last March 19.

Hot Springs has received too much unfavorable publicity in the past as being a refuge and hideout for criminals and gangsters. It has largely outgrown that reputation in recent years except for the occasional furor over Frank Costello's visits. We hold no brief for Costello, but at least he has never been charged with a crime of violence, and we can see no parallel between his sojourns here as a tourist, and having Anastasia, reputed head of a "slay for pay" organization, come here as a permanent or temporary resident.

Hot Springs must not become the dumping ground for the scum of the underworld.

If Albert Anastasia, reputed "lord high executioner" of Murder, Inc., intends coming to Hot Springs to avoid being rubbed out by gangland's guns, as reported in the Associated Press in New York yesterday, he'll find no welcome mat spread out for him.

"We're not going to have him here," declared Circuit Judge C. Floyd Huff, Jr. bluntly when informed the Brooklyn waterfront boss was planning to "retire" to this nationally famous health resort.

"If he thinks he can run away from New York mobsters and run down here, he'd better think again," said Judge Huff. "He can do his running in some other direction."

He said if there were some legitimate excuse for his coming—to take the baths, for instance, for the benefit of his health—it might be different.

(Recently Frank Costello, reputed gambling kingpin of the nation, visited Hot Springs with permission of the federal court, to take the baths, for arthritis. He has been here frequently in the past.)

Assistant Chief of Police John Ermey opined that "he (Anastasia) might retire in one of our city jail cells until he changed his mind about staying here. It would be easy enough to place a vagrancy charge against him and move him on his way."

Prosecuting Attorney R. Julian Glover said, "I do not want anyone here of doubtful character. That includes Anastasia."

Sheriff Will Lowe was frank to admit that he'd never heard of Anastasia, accused of working "double cross"—gangdom's highest crime—with Willie Moretti, another eastern hoodlum, but said "It won't be any trouble to get rid of him should he show up here. We can get him out of town quickly enough."

Moretti was slain Oct. 4 in Cliffside Park, N.J. restaurant ...

The last bathhouse to be authorized by the US Department of the Interior was the Jack Tar Hotel and Bath House (above). The modern, luxurious, five-story structure was located on Oriole Street off Park Avenue. Across Park Avenue was the Rainbow Room, a large white building decorated with multicolored neon tubing. Both the hotel and lounge had been built by a Galveston, Texas, friend of Frank Costello. In 1949, Costello bought an interest in the hotel when his friend needed money for expansion. It was rumored that another friend of Costello's, Jimmy Hoffa, was involved in the bankrolling. Hoffa was also rumored to have built the Aristocrat Hotel, at 240 Central Avenue, across from the Arlington Hotel, to provide a casino for Teamsters Union members to enjoy. The Aristocrat (below), in addition to having a grand showroom, also contained a glass-bottomed swimming pool above the lobby. (Courtesy of GCHS.)

Owney Madden loved spending time with Meyer Lansky (shown here). Lansky, like Madden, was not considered a member of the Mafia, but was part of a close circle of non-Italians who served as consultants and advisers. Madden especially enjoyed getting news from New York from Lansky, Luciano, and Costello that he could not get from his daily reading of the *New York Times*. (Courtesy of GCHS.)

Meyer Lansky would also visit the spa city to get treatment at the Leo N. Levi Hospital for his oldest son, Bernard Irving "Buddy" Lansky (1930–1989), who was permanently disabled with cerebral palsy. The hospital opened in 1914 at 318 Prospect Avenue, offering free care. In 1936, the hospital established an arthritis-study program using the thermal waters of the springs. By the 1960s, Levi was recognized as one of the top arthritis treatment centers in the country. (Courtesy of GCHS.)

H. Dane Harris (left) was the third and final gambling czar of Hot Springs. He was preceded by Jack McJunkins and, prior to that, by boss gambler W.S. Jacobs. Harris brought to the city a modern vision for nightlife. His idea was to hire top-notch entertainment, world-class chefs, and professionally trained dealers to provide a venue that would compete with Las Vegas. Hot Springs for years had attracted East Coast, Texas, and Louisiana gamblers, and Harris courted them like they were his first love. The club he opened at 315 Park Avenue, the Vapors (above), was a regular stop for performers like Tony Bennett, Phyllis Diller, Jerry Van Dyke, Patti Page, Liberace, and Mickey Rooney, to name a few. In 1965, the Vapors was the site for Owen Madden's wake. (Courtesy of Mark Palmer.)

The gambling parlor of the Vapors nightclub housed roulette, blackjack, and craps tables, as well as slot machines. The slots were a product of Spa Amusement, a company owned by Dane Harris and his partners. An adjacent room, the Monte Carlo, was the entertainment venue for the club and was flanked by a coffee shop and grill. (Courtesy of Historical Attractions Inc.)

Few noticed, and even fewer cared, that the first escalator in Arkansas, located in the Southern Club, would only transport guests upward. If one wanted to leave the club, he would have to traverse downwards via the marble staircase. Some Hot Springs natives say that a lot of people came just to ride the escalator. (Courtesy of Historical Attractions Inc.)

The backbone of any mechanical operation is the mechanic himself. In the case of the Spa Amusement Company, Ernie Bone and Tony Frazier were given the responsibility of keeping over 600 slots operating smoothly and, most of all, producing cash. Their task was complicated by people who did not want to wait for their number to come up, and so cheated the machines. (Courtesy of Harley Bone.)

In the late 1950s, the mechanics at the Spa Amusement Company developed what they believed were crook-proof machines that would no longer allow someone to slip a device into the slot, thus holding open the jackpot. The new machine was called the Spa Bell. While it passed the test against the cheaters, it could not escape the jaws of the law. (Courtesy of Harley Bone.)

One of the many members of the Chicago Outfit who continued to visit Hot Springs long after Big Al Capone had gone for good was Sam "Momo" Giancana. In the early 1960s, Giancana found his way back to Hot Springs. During a Maguire Sisters' engagement at the Vapors nightclub, he had FBI resident agent Clay White watching his every move. According to some family members of the Hot Springs gambling community, Giancana attempted to buy an interest in the spa city action. While the local partners of profit had once entertained the idea of inviting Frank Costello to run their show, they had no problem turning away Sam Giancana. (Right, courtesy of Argenta Images; below, courtesy of Corbis Images.)

Oaklawn Thoroughbred Race Track was opened by the owners of the Southern Club in 1905. It was one of two horse racetracks in Hot Springs, the other being Essex Park. Both tracks were closed between 1907 and 1917 due to anti-gambling laws. Essex burned down in 1917, the day after its grand reopening, leaving Oaklawn the only game in town. It, too, closed intermittently due to persistent legislation prohibiting gambling. In 1934, the newly formed Business Men's Racing

Association, which included Mayor McLaughlin, hosted a day at the races, and a portion of the proceeds was delivered to the Arkansas state capitol as a voluntary sales tax. Soon thereafter, the betting windows at Oaklawn reopened and remain open to this day. Oaklawn Park is the largest single taxpayer in Arkansas. (Courtesy of Fred Mark Palmer.)

It's not what you do but how you do it!
Maxine, 1954

Grace Goldstein was the most famous madam in Hot Springs until the early 1950s, when Maxine Harris Jones rolled into town in her Cadillac convertible. Jones started her career in Texarkana, Arkansas, as a prostitute, but soon learned that she was entertaining clients who were on their way to a bigger party, and that party was in Hot Springs. Realizing where the money was, she rented a place on Prospect Avenue just off Central Avenue, hired a couple of girls, and began marketing her product. By the time the late 1950s rolled around, she had two small bordellos and a large house of "extreme pleasure" that she called the mansion (below). She advertised her business by putting her new girls, sporting inviting smiles, upon the back of her convertible and riding down Central Avenue, parade-style. (Left, courtesy of Marti Devasher; below, courtesy GCHS.)

Seven

THE END OF THE GAME

Nestled in a lush, green valley of the Ouachita Mountains in central Arkansas, within an echo of three beautiful deepwater lakes and cold-water rivers, lies the sleepy little resort town of Hot Springs. A big difference between this resort town and other resort towns is that, according to the FBI, it had by 1964 grown into a $100-million-a-year gambling operation. The only problem: gambling was against the law. Gambling never was, nor is it today, legal in Arkansas.

Over the years, the people of Hot Springs have endured some of the most catastrophic events in Arkansas history. Three major fires, in 1878, 1905, and 1913, destroyed most or all of the downtown business district. Following each disaster, the citizens picked up the pieces and started over. Their resolve was as predictable as the water that flowed from the cracks in the earth. Water flooded Central Avenue many times over the years, destroying businesses. But, again, the citizens' strength prevailed, and they mopped up and marched on.

The Army marched into Hot Springs during World War II, commandeering the city's two largest hotels to serve as rehabilitation centers for returning soldiers. Another hotel, the Park, was used as a prisoner-of-war camp for German officers. Following the war, a group of returning GIs overthrew the existing political machine of Leo McLaughlin. They attempted to rebuild the reputation of the city without gambling, but the moratorium lasted only a short while. With the popularity of bathing and hot thermal baths drying up, partly due to advances made in the pharmaceutical industry, and comforted by the fact that they had survived the McLaughlin era, the new administration would reorganize and once again roll the dice. Gambling seemed to be the only hope for prosperity for the city, but it would not be a hit right off the bat. The GI administration split into two factions, one for and one against gambling. Sid McMath, the founder of the GI Revolt, successfully ran for governor. Unsure of his cooperation, gambling interests went into backrooms. Oaklawn Park Race Track continued to grow in popularity, as betting on horses was not considered gambling according to Arkansas law. Eventually, a new political regime took over, and Hot Springs regained its wide-open status. A new gambling czar was appointed, and the gangsters began to return to their favorite retreat like the swallows to Capistrano.

Meanwhile, Estes Kefauver, who had been a high school math teacher in Hot Springs many years earlier, was conducting Senate hearings on organized crime, casting a dark shadow on the Valley of the Vapors. About the only thing admitted by any member of organized crime who testified in the hearings was that they vacationed in Hot Springs. The rest of the time, they pled the Fifth Amendment. Escaping the wrath of Congress, the roulette wheels of the spa city continued to spin. After all, Owney Madden still lived in Hot Springs and was doing quite well. In the late 1950s, Madden operated one of the largest sport books in the country, along with his interest in the clubs. New hotels and plush casinos were being built, but Hot Springs would soon face a series of events from which recovery would be questionable.

Once again, things were heating up in Washington, DC, concerning the spa city and its link to the mob. Bobby Kennedy, appointed special counsel for the newly formed McClellan Senate subcommittee hearings on organized crime, began fighting for new federal laws governing interstate commerce, including telephone and telegraph wire services.

But while getting clean and healthy in a hot thermal bath was a thing of the past, the fate of getting down and dirty on the blackjack tables of Hot Springs was still in the hands of the state; and that action would be safe as long as Orval Faubus was getting his share of the monthly profit. Serving his fifth two-year term as governor of Arkansas in 1964, Faubus, like most governors before him (with the exception of Carl Bailey, Homer Adkins, and Sid McMath), seemed to look the other way in matters of illegal gambling. Reform groups were gaining recognition among some politicians, especially a multimillionaire Republican candidate, Winthrop Rockefeller, who had narrowly been defeated by Faubus in the previous election. During that campaign, Faubus fired a shot across the bow of the Hot Springs gambling establishment by conducting a few cursory raids on the casinos. It was an attempt to satisfy the opponents of Hot Springs' only industry, gambling.

Big-name entertainers continued to put Hot Springs on their booking calendars. Many movers and shakers thought that the shows and fine dining would make the gambling more palatable to the local citizens. It did, to a certain extent; but it also attracted new mob bosses, like Sam Giancana.

In 1965, Owen Vincent Madden, former beer baron of New York City and arguably the backbone of the Hot Springs gambling industry, died. Madden and his wife had been supporters of Rockefeller, who won the 1966 gubernatorial election.

When Winthrop Rockefeller took office in 1967, it is reported that he spoke to state senator Q. Byrum Hurst Sr. and other legislators in regard to the gambling in Hot Springs. He said that if they, as legislators, were able to get a gambling amendment passed, he would not stand in its way. The Arkansas legislature passed an amendment to legalize gambling in 1967, but, shortly before the bill was to go into law, it was vetoed by Rockefeller. Later that year, raids were conducted and illegal gambling came to a close in the spa city. Some historians theorize that Rockefeller's veto was forced on him by his brother Nelson and the Las Vegas mob. Many of these historians are also under the impression that the mob was always in control of things in Hot Springs, and that local control was only a facade.

Today, like so many times before, Hot Springs, Arkansas, has seized victory from the jaws of defeat. It is a thriving mecca of tourism without legalized gambling. The hot water continues to flow, taking a thermal bath is back in vogue, and the rich history of its gangster past attracts visitors from all over the world, strolling the sidewalks of Central Avenue and Bathhouse Row.

Disasters have been as big a part of Hot Springs history as the notorious, rich, and famous visitors to the city. Major fires destroyed over 1,000 buildings each in 1905 and 1913. In addition, Hot Springs Creek, now rolling beneath Central Avenue, has pushed water inside the buildings that line the avenue several times through history. The below photograph, taken during one of the catastrophic fires that raged through the downtown area, includes, oddly enough, the Terminal Hotel. Hot Springs would never use the word "terminal" when discussing its future. (Above, courtesy of Mary D. Hudgins Collection, Special Collections, University of Arkansas Libraries, Fayetteville; below, courtesy of GCHS.)

Sen. John F. Kennedy (seated, center) attended the Arkansas Bar Conference at the Arlington Hotel in 1957. He is seen here with former mayor Leo P. McLaughlin (seated, right). The senator, by this time, had become used to downplaying or side-stepping questions about his father, Joseph Kennedy. Years before, Joseph had visited Hot Springs and Oklahoma to procure moonshine whiskey. In what might be called a strange twist of fate, a manager of a nationally syndicated beauty parlor was asked by Owney Madden to groom a friend of his on a Sunday, which was not a normal business day for the manager. The client told her: "Make me look good, because I'm going to be on television next week. The beautician accommodated him, and, one week later, discovered the name of her client, Jack Ruby, when he did indeed appear on television, shooting Lee Harvey Oswald. (Courtesy of Mary D. Hudgins Collection. Special Collections, University of Arkansas Libraries, Fayetteville.)

The talk around the water cooler at the Arkansas state capitol in 1967 was how Orval Eugene Faubus could afford to buy 240 acres on a mountain and build a mansion designed by famed architect Faye Jones on the $10,000 salary he received as governor. Most suspected that one had to look no further than 40 miles to the southwest of the capitol, to Hot Springs, to allay their curiosity. Faubus, a six-term governor, had been looking the other way when it came to enforcing the antigambling laws in Arkansas. He claimed he had been saving his money, and, in fact, he did establish a foundation that would set up cash donations to his building fund. In the above photograph, Faubus (right) is at Oaklawn Race Track with the first of his three wives, Alta (center). (Above, courtesy of Historical Attractions Inc.; below, courtesy of Special Collections, University of Arkansas, Fayetteville.)

Winthrop Rockefeller was the fifth of six children born to John D. Rockefeller Jr., of the Rockefeller Standard Oil dynasty, founded by Winthrop's grandfather, John D. Rockefeller Sr. He came to Arkansas in 1953, quickly establishing firm roots in the state, particularly in west central Arkansas on Petit Jean Mountain. He became the first Republican governor in Arkansas since Reconstruction. Winthrop Rockefeller will always be remembered, not for the economic development he brought to the state, but for the termination of open, illegal gambling in Hot Springs. He was supported in his bid for governor by several members of the Hot Springs gambling community. However, after his veto of the gambling amendment, he would not serve another term as governor. (Left, courtesy of Special Collections, University of Arkansas, Fayetteville; below, courtesy of Rockefeller Collection, UALR.)

AN URGENT REQUEST

To The

CITIZENS of ARKANSAS

As you know, the gamblers have managed to ramrod through the legislature a bill to legalize casino gambling. This is in direct conflict with the will of the people as overwhelmngly expressed in the 1964 election.

Nevada is the only state with legalized casino gambling, and it has the highest crime rate in the entire country.

Governor Rockefeller now holds our destiny in his hands. HE CAN KILL THE BILL WITH HIS VETO, or he can allow it to become a law by simply refusing to sign it.

IF YOU CARE ANYTHING AT ALL ABOUT YOUR FAMILY AND YOUR STATE, THEN IMMEDIATELY URGE THE GOVERNOR TO VETO THIS BILL.

WE ONLY HAVE 5 DAYS, SO PLEASE ACT IMMEDIATELY

C. U. A. G.

CHURCHES UNITED AGAINST GAMBLING

Pol. Adv. Paid For By James B. Gannaway, Chairman

Reformists, as they were called by the gamblers in the spa city, were gathering momentum in their drive to eradicate what they considered sin. This campaign flyer proclaims: "As you know, the gamblers have managed to ramrod through the legislature a bill to legalize casino gambling. This is in direct conflict with the will of the people as overwhelmingly expressed in the 1964 election. Nevada is the only state with legalized casino gambling, and it has the highest crime rate in the entire country. Governor Rockefeller now holds our destiny in his hands. HE CAN KILL THE BILL WITH HIS VETO, or he can allow it to become a law by simply refusing to sign it. IF YOU CARE ANYTHING AT ALL ABOUT YOUR FAMILY AND YOUR STATE, THEN IMMEDIATELY URGE THE GOVERNOR TO VETO THIS BILL." (Courtesy of Fred Mark Palmer.)

In the dining halls of the grand hotels that stand in the Valley of the Vapors, lavish dining was part of the Hot Springs experience, especially when one had old friends in town. Shown here, at a dinner hosted by Owen and Agnes Madden, are undefeated heavyweight champion Rocky Marciano (at the head of the table), Q. Byrum Hurst Sr. (to Marciano's right), and mayor Floyd Housley. (Courtesy of Fred Mark Palmer.)

Rocky Marciano visited Hot Springs often, exploring opportunities in real estate ventures. Owney Madden was instrumental in Marciano's transition from the world of boxing into his post-fighting life. Marciano, seen here with Fred Mark Palmer (right) on July 4, 1969, at Belvedere Golf and Country Club, continued to visit Hot Springs even after Madden's death. On August 31, 1969, Marciano was killed in a plane crash in Iowa. (Courtesy of Fred Mark Palmer.)

In the spring of 1961, famed crooner Tony Bennett pulled into Hot Springs with his accompanist, legendary jazz pianist Ralph Sharon, for an engagement at The Vapors nightclub. Following the performance, they left the Velda Rose Hotel, where they were staying, and walked down to The Black Orchid nightclub at 128 Central Avenue. Once inside, using the piano at the bar, the two musicians decided to go over some sheet music they had received from a composer while they were in New York City. Bennett soulfully sang "I Left My Heart in San Francisco." After the initial run-through of the piece, bartender C.B. Hudson, who was the only other person in the club at the time, told the duo that he really liked the song, and he would buy it if they decided to record it. The rest is history, and it became Bennett's signature song. Over 40 years later, in 2003, Tony Bennett returned to the spa city and performed the song, this time to the sold-out crowd at the grand opening of the Summit Arena. (Courtesy of Don Hunstein, © Sony Music Entertainment.)

William Jefferson Clinton moved to Hot Springs with his parents, Roger and Virginia, in 1950 at the age of four. He quickly settled in to life in "Sin City," as he refers to the town in his biography. Clinton recalled that he would walk from his house on Park Avenue, down Central Avenue and Bathhouse Row, to attend band practice at Hot Springs High School. (Courtesy of GCHS.)

Clinton is shown with his good friend and classmate Paul David Leopoulos in a play at Hot Springs High School. Their friendship began in grade school and continues to this day. Little did anyone know that this would not be the last stage on which Clinton would perform. Leopoulos recognized early on that Clinton was "an exceptional, intellectual people person." (Courtesy of GCHS.)

Patrons of The Vapors nightclub packed the house when Phyllis Diller came to town. Her sharp wit and comedic timing were punctuated with her trademark burst of laughter. Unlike other acts, who brought their bands with them, Phyllis hired local musicians to accompany her. Audiences as well as the musicians were surprised when she showed off her skills at the piano. (Courtesy of Fred Mark Palmer.)

The Ames Brothers were known for their deep, smooth voices and harmonies. Three of the brothers are shown in this photograph, taken at the Belvedere in the 1960s, when all four brothers performed there. They performed on some occasions with the Maguire Sisters. Vic Ames became the entertainment director for the Belvedere and The Vapors. (Courtesy of Historical Attractions Inc.)

In a 20-minute eulogy, state senator Q. Byrum Hurst of Hot Springs described Owen Madden as "a very cherished friend to everything good in this community. Whenever a person was down on his luck, he knew that a helping hand would be found in Owen Madden. " Hurst said that Madden had given standing orders to the help at a local restaurant to give anyone a meal who was hungry and could not afford it. And Madden paid for it. "This community was Owen Madden's home, and you were his friends and neighbors—and he loved you. If Owen made a dollar, it was rapidly given to someone else who needed it more. . . . There is no ball park named after Owen Madden, no silver cup bearing his name, but his name is written upon the hearts of all the people he helped—with money, by deed, and by word of encouragement in their dark hours. It has been said that there is so much good in the worst of us, and so much bad in the best of us, that it doesn't behoove any of us to criticize the rest of us." (Courtesy of Q. Byrum Hurst Jr.)

The newspaper article shown at right includes the following passage: "Owen Vincent (Owney) Madden, aged 73, a New York underworld figure of the prohibition era, died at 12:10 a.m. Saturday at a hospital here. Death was attributed to chronic emphysema, a lung disease. Madden had been dubbed by police as the 'Clay Pigeon' because he had been riddled with bullets many times during his racketeer days in New York and New Jersey. He was involved in six slaying investigations but served only two prison terms—one for 'instigating' the killing of Little Patsy Doyle and the other for parole violation. While in Sing Sing Prison, he admitted to operating a brewery in New York that turned out 300,000 gallons of beer a day." (Right, courtesy of Mary D. Hudgins Collection, Special Collections, University of Arkansas Libraries, Fayetteville; below, courtesy of Historical Attractions Inc.)

Col. Lynn Davis, as he was referred to during his service as director of the Arkansas State Police, was born in Texarkana, Arkansas. He joined the FBI after attending Henderson State University in Arkadelphia, Arkansas, and served in the robbery and homicide division in Los Angeles, California. Agent Davis requested and was granted a transfer to the Little Rock office by J. Edgar Hoover. Davis was contacted by a spokesman for the newly elected governor of Arkansas, Winthrop Rockefeller, and asked if he would take the job as the head of the Arkansas State Police. He was also asked if he had the courage to close the casinos in Hot Springs. Rockefeller warned Davis that it might be the hardest thing he would ever do in his career, because closing down the largest illegal gambling operation in America had been tried many times before, resulting only in failure. Davis told the governor, "I will enforce the law to its fullest extent." He got the job, and, at the age of 34, Lynn Arthur Davis was about to make Arkansas history. (Courtesy of Arkansas State Police.)

Col. Lynn Davis thought he had devised a perfect plan for putting a stop to the illegal gambling in Hot Springs. His plan was to simply confiscate the gambling equipment and leave the owners and their money alone. On the night of October 17, 1967, Davis positioned his state troopers outside many of the larger clubs and called the municipal judge to obtain search warrants. The judge told Davis that it would be best for him to come down to the office about 9:30 in the morning, and that the judge would make that happen. Davis told the judge, "That will be fine, we've got the clubs surrounded front and back. My state troopers have taken over the city." The judge replied, "I'll be down in five minutes." The plan worked perfectly. Or, at least, it seemed. The next morning, Colonel Davis turned the confiscated equipment, slot machines, roulette tables, dice tables, and card tables over to the Hot Springs Police Department. Within two weeks, though, the equipment was back in the hands of the gamblers. The clubs were back in business. (Courtesy of Arkansas State Police.)

Upon the clubs' reopening after Davis's raids, Governor Rockefeller's phone began to ring. The governor summoned Davis back to Hot Springs to finish the job, and he did. Tons of gambling equipment was destroyed and buried in gravel pits around the city or smashed with bulldozers and hauled off. Colonel Davis estimated that in his first raid, he had left about $10 million in the counting rooms of the Hot Springs casinos. Oddly enough, Davis was the only one arrested in the whole affair. He was summoned by the grand jury and asked to identify his informant. When he refused, he was held in contempt. A few days later, Rockefeller's team of lawyers went to the Arkansas Supreme Court, and Davis was freed. (Courtesy of Historical Attractions Inc.)

Bill and Tyler Seiz of Seiz Sign & Neon Company dismantle the last vestige of the Hot Springs gambling glory days, removing the neon dancing showgirl and the sign from the front of the Southern Club. A Canadian firm subsequently leased the building for a wax museum. In stark contrast, the lively action that once transpired behind the doors of the club was replaced by the frozen poses of figures in wax. Following the removal of the sign, an auction was held. An article that appeared in the *Hot Springs New Era* on February 15, 1971, states: "One observer remarked that the 'entire Arkansas syndicate' had collected at the auction and solemnly observed the sale of kitchen equipment, dishes, tables, chairs and even parts of the bar. He estimated that 500 persons were there. As the observer phrased it, the former gamblers had come to 'pay their respects.' " (Courtesy of Fred Mark Palmer.)

Özel türkbaş

Some of the more enterprising members of the gambling community were not quite finished with their venture when Governor Rockefeller whacked illegal gambling. A group of businessmen decided to take their knowledge of the game and their money overseas. They acquired a palace on the shore of the Strait of Istanbul in Turkey and called it Casino D'Istanbul. For years, it was operated using former spa city casino employees, flying both the profit and the last shift home to Hot Springs every 30 days. In 1975, the casino closed with the threat of Turkish government intervention on the horizon. (Courtesy of Mike Ellis.)

Summer palace of former Prime Minister Sait Halim Pasna now Casino D'Istanbul only minutes away from downtown Istanbul.

Casino D'Istanbul
Sait Halim Paşa Yalısı
P.O. Box. 16 Yeniköy, İstanbul. Turkéy
Cable Address : THECASİNO, Yeniköy-İSTANBUL
Telephone : 63 68 22

GÜZEL SANATLAR MATBAASI A.Ş.

When these old friends got together in Hot Springs, many a reporter would have paid to have been a fly on the wall. Leonard Ellis (left), the son of a doctor, was the high sheriff of Garland County, and a stockholder in the Belvedere and Casino D'Istanbul. Sid McMath (center), son of a farmer, was a decorated war hero, a prosecuting attorney of Hot Springs, and a governor of Arkansas. Q. Byrum Hurst Sr. (right), son of a preacher, was an attorney, veteran, state senator, and special counsel to Owen Madden. They fought the enemy and won in World War II, and they fought Leo McLaughlin and won in Hot Springs. They even fought with each other from time to time, but they felt they won, because, through it all, they remained friends. Hot Springs, Arkansas, is a better place due to their efforts. (Courtesy of Mike Ellis.)

In 1964, during a gubernatorial election year that brought about a temporary gambling shutdown, an article published in the *Saturday Evening Post* by John Skow read: "Civic virtue is not the first thing that leaps to mind at the mention of Hot Springs, Arkansas, a sedately sinful little resort town in the Ouachita Mountains. . . . Just now, however, Hot Springs is a disaster area. . . . Until a few months ago, Hot Springs had been green—an elegant oasis for those who enjoyed gracious wagering—almost without a break since Civil War days." When gambling came to a close in Hot Springs in 1967, everyone thought the end was near; but the spa city lives on. Millions of tourists come to the Valley of the Vapors each year to stroll down Bathhouse Row and to walk in the footsteps of the rich, the famous, the powerful, and the notorious; and yes, of course, to take hot thermal baths in the healing waters of the hot springs. (Courtesy of Hot Springs Convention Center.)

ACKNOWLEDGMENTS

I wish to thank the University of Arkansas Libraries, Fayetteville, caretakers of the Mary D. Hudgins Collection, and especially Tim Nutt and his staff, Geoffery Stark and Megan Massanelli. The collection was a major contributor of images for this book.

Thanks also to the Garland County Historical Society (GCHS), led by executive director Elizabeth Robbins and her staff. Their tireless devotion to the preservation of all things Hot Springs should be a model for every city in the nation.

I also wish to thank my team at Arcadia Publishing: Jason Humphrey, Maggie Bullwinkel, Joe Walker, and Jim Kempert. Their patience and guidance through the process of creating this work, and their dedication to the consistent high quality of the product, sets a standard for American publishing.

Several individuals provided invaluable knowledge from their personal research, expertise, and passion for the history of Hot Springs and its visitors. Specifically, I wish to thank Orval Allbritton, Isabel Anthony, Dr. Dee Brown, Joe Demby, Ray Griffin Jr., William J. Helmer, Todd Marchese, Lee Muncy Jr., Fred Mark Palmer, the *Hot Springs Sentinel Record*, Wayne Threadgill, and Clay White.

My gratitude extends to the staff of the Gangster Museum of America, Hot Springs Convention Center and Visitors Bureau director Steve Arrison, Ed Attwater, Deirdre Marie Capone, Morris Cash, Colonel Lynn Davis, Walter Ebel, Mike Ellis, Bill Foster, Antoinette Giancana, Rosalie Watt Harkins, Paul Hastings, Q. Byrum Hurst Jr., Meyer Lansky II, Granger McDaniel Jr., Sandy McMath, Esther Muncrief, Norwood Phillips, Nate Robinson, Gene Stonecipher, Billy Wells, and James Ev Young.

This book would never have seen the light of day without the tolerance and skills of the following: Ann Raines, Adam Raines, Katie Raines, Elizabeth Brockman, Betsy Westbrook Burrow, and Tommy Priakos. Finally, to my wife, Ann: thank you for the patience and love needed to live with an entrepreneur.

BIBLIOGRAPHY

Allbritton, Orval E. *Dangerous Visitors, the Lawless Era*. Delight, AR: Garland County Historical Society, Alexander Printing Company, 2008.

———. *The Mob at the Spa: Organized Crime and Its Fascination with Hot Springs, Arkansas*. Delight, AR: Garland County Historical Society, Alexander Printing Company, 2011.

Helmer, William J. *The Gun that Made the Twenties Roar*. New York: Macmillan Publishing Co., 1969.

Helmer, William J., and Rick Mattix. *The Complete Public Enemy Almanac*. Nashville, TN: Cumberland House Publishing Inc., 2007.

Poulson, Ellen, *The Case Against Lucky Luciano: New York's Most Sensational Vice Trial*. Oakland Gardens, NY: Clinton Cook Publishing, 2007.

Raines, Robert, ed. *7, Seven Historic Articles That Chronicle the Colorful Past of America's First Resort*. Hot Springs, AR: Historic Arkansas Productions, 2012.

DISCOVER THOUSANDS OF LOCAL HISTORY BOOKS FEATURING MILLIONS OF VINTAGE IMAGES

Arcadia Publishing, the leading local history publisher in the United States, is committed to making history accessible and meaningful through publishing books that celebrate and preserve the heritage of America's people and places.

Find more books like this at
www.arcadiapublishing.com

Search for your hometown history, your old stomping grounds, and even your favorite sports team.